Introductions to the Books of the Bible

By the
Daughters of St. Paul

Foreword by
Most Reverend Lawrence J. Riley, S.T.D.

ST. PAUL EDITIONS

NIHIL OBSTAT:
Rev. Thomas Buckley, STD, SSL

IMPRIMATUR:
✠ Humberto Cardinal Medeiros
Archbishop of Boston

Scripture texts used in this work not indicated by an asterisk are taken from the *New American Bible,* copyright © 1970, by the Confraternity of Christian Doctrine, Washington, D.C., and are used by permission of copyright owner. All rights reserved.

The Scripture quotations in this publication indicated by one asterisk (*) are from the *Revised Standard Version Bible* (modified form), Catholic Edition, copyrighted © 1965 and 1966 by the Division of Christian Education of the National Council of the Churches of Christ in the U.S.A., and used by permission.

Scripture texts indicated by two asterisks (**) are from *The Jerusalem Bible,* copyright © 1966 by Darton, Longman & Todd, Ltd. and Doubleday and Company, Inc. Used by permission of the publisher.

Library of Congress Cataloging in Publication Data

Daughters of St. Paul.
   Introductions to the books of the Bible.

   1. Bible—Introductions. I. Title.
BS475.2.D37   1982   220.7   81-19556
                                          AACR2
ISBN 0-8198-3605-2 (cloth)
      0-8198-3606-0 (paper)

Copyright © 1982, by the Daughters of St. Paul

Printed in the U.S.A. by the Daughters of St. Paul
50 St. Paul's Ave., Boston, MA 02130

The Daughters of St. Paul are an international congregation of religious women serving the Church with the communications media.

CONTENTS

Foreword	11
God's Book and Ours	13
The Voice of the Popes	14
Before Reading Sacred Scripture	16
After Reading Sacred Scripture	16
Introduction	17
God's Message to Us	17
Sacred Scripture and Sacred Tradition	19
The Bible—A Sacred Library!	21
When? Where? In What Languages?	26
Texts and Versions	27
Chapters and Verses	28
Inspiration and Inerrancy	28
The Interpretation of Scripture	29
The Science of Interpretation	32
How Should We Read Scripture?	34
The Geography of the Holy Land	35
Some Highlights of Palestinian History	37

THE OLD TESTAMENT

The Old Testament	41
The Pentateuch	43
The Book of Genesis	46
The Book of Exodus	50
The Book of Leviticus	53
The Book of Numbers	55
The Book of Deuteronomy	57
The Book of Joshua	60
The Book of Judges	63
The Book of Ruth	65
The First and Second Books of Samuel	67
The First and Second Books of Kings	71
The First and Second Books of Chronicles	74
The Books of Ezra and Nehemiah	79
The Book of Tobit	84
The Book of Judith	89

The Book of Esther	92
The First and Second Books of Maccabees	95
The Book of Job	100
The Book of Psalms	102
The Book of Proverbs	120
The Book of Ecclesiastes	122
The Song of Songs	124
The Book of Wisdom	126
The Book of Sirach or Ecclesiasticus	128
The Prophets	130
The Book of Isaiah	136
The Book of Jeremiah	139
The Book of Lamentations	141
The Book of Baruch	142
The Book of Ezekiel	143
The Book of Daniel	146
The Book of Hosea	148
The Book of Joel	149
The Book of Amos	149
The Book of Obadiah	150
The Book of Jonah	150
The Book of Micah	151
The Book of Nahum	152
The Book of Habakkuk	152
The Book of Zephaniah	153
The Book of Haggai	154
The Book of Zechariah	155
The Book of Malachi	156

THE NEW TESTAMENT

The New Testament	161
The Gospel According to St. Matthew	163
The Gospel According to St. Mark	167
The Gospel According to St. Luke	170
The Gospel According to St. John	173
The Acts of the Apostles	176
The Letter of Paul to the Romans	179
The First Letter of Paul to the Corinthians	185
The Second Letter of Paul to the Corinthians	187
The Letter of Paul to the Galatians	189
The Letter of Paul to the Ephesians	192
The Letter of Paul to the Philippians	195

The Letter of Paul to the Colossians	197
The First Letter of Paul to the Thessalonians	199
The Second Letter of Paul to the Thessalonians	201
The Letters of Paul to Timothy and Titus	202
The Letter of Paul to Philemon	205
The Letter to the Hebrews	206
The Letter of James	209
The First Letter of Peter	211
The Second Letter of Peter	213
The First Letter of John	214
The Second and Third Letters of John	215
The Letter of Jude	216
The Book of Revelation	217
Bible Passages for Particular Needs	219
Special Psalms for Special Needs	221
Bibliography	223

Foreword

Someone once wrote that as Christ is the King of kings and the Lord of lords, so the Bible is the Book of books. It is God's book of revelation. He is its principal Author. In the Old Testament are recorded the promise and the expectation of the Messiah, as well as the history of the Chosen People from whom the Messiah was to be born. The New Testament presents the life and teaching of the Messiah, Jesus Christ, the Son of God, and sketches the history of the early Church.

No one can ever fully evaluate the enormous impact that the Bible has had on the religious, spiritual and moral life of the human race. Even today, as is evidenced by a recent Gallup Poll, Bible reading is considered to be the single most discernible factor shaping moral behavior, both on a personal level and on a social level.

Very beautifully has the Second Vatican Council declared that "the Church has always venerated the divine Scriptures as she venerated the Body of the Lord, insofar as she never ceases, particularly in the sacred liturgy, to partake of the bread of life and to offer it to the faithful from the one table of the Word of God and the Body of Christ." The Council is almost lyrical in its description of the Bible. "In the sacred books the Father who is in heaven comes lovingly to meet His children, and talks with them. And such is the force and power of the Word of God that it can serve the Church as her support and vigor, and the children of the Church as strength for their faith, food for the soul, and a pure and lasting fount of spiritual life."

Reading the Bible will obviously be much more meaningful when one knows something of its background and has a deeper knowledge of the historical context of the particular book in question, together with an appreciation of the literary style of its human author.

Moreover, such reading can be a rich source of spiritual nourishment when the lessons to be derived from Sacred Scripture are applied to day-to-day living.

There is no dearth of excellent and erudite volumes on the Bible for scholars and academicians who are interested in the history of the times in which the various books of the Bible were written, as well as in the rigidly scientific aspects of biblical study and of biblical theology. In the present volume there are offered to the public more popular, but no less accurate *Introductions to the Books of the Bible*. Despite the brevity of this volume it is surprisingly comprehensive. Its potential for good is truly immeasurable. Simply and clearly written, it meets a definite need. It is surely a response to the urging of the Second Vatican Council that "access to Sacred Scripture ought to be open wide to the Christian faithful."

In the final analysis, an assessment of the value of a book such as this will depend upon the answers to two questions: Does the book help me better to understand the Bible, and does it contribute to my spiritual growth? In the case of *Introductions to the Books of the Bible* the reader will find that this volume admirably performs both functions. May it have the wide circulation that it truly deserves.

✠Lawrence J. Riley, S.T.D.
Auxiliary Bishop of Boston

GOD'S BOOK AND OURS

How the Word of God Works

"Yes, as the rain and the snow come down from the heavens and do not return without watering the earth, making it yield and giving growth to provide seed for the sower and bread for the eating, so the word that goes from my mouth does not return to me empty, without carrying out my will and succeeding in what it was sent to do" (Is. 55:10-11).**

The Sign of the New Times

"See what days are coming—it is the Lord Yahweh
    who speaks—
days when I will bring famine on the country, a famine not of bread, a drought not of water, but of hearing the word of Yahweh" (Am. 8:11).**

Sweetness of the Word of God

" 'Son of man, feed and be satisfied by the scroll I am giving you.' I ate it, and it tasted sweet as honey" (Ez. 3:3).**

THE VOICE OF THE POPES

Pope John XXIII

The Bible in Every Home

"This is our goal, this is our program: the Bible in every family."

"Today for a self-respecting Christian, ignorance of the Bible is unpardonable. Ignorance of the Scriptures is, in fact, ignorance of Christ."

"If all the solicitudes of the pastoral ministries are dear to us, and we realize their urgency, above all we feel the duty of enkindling everywhere and continuously enthusiasm for every manifestation of the Divine Book."

Pope Paul VI

A Necessary Return

"It is necessary to return to the Bible: it will never be recommended enough that we nourish our faith at this awe-inspiring font. Our spiritual life often is nourished by reading works written by men, certainly learned and holy, but not directly inspired by God like the authors of the Bible were."

"We can only say we are truly Christians when the Word of God becomes our pattern for living."

Pope John Paul II

Catechesis and the Bible

"Catechesis will always draw its content from the living source of the Word of God transmitted in Tradition and the Scriptures, for "Sacred Tradition and Sacred Scripture make up a single sacred deposit of the Word of God, which is entrusted to the Church."

"To speak of Tradition and Scripture as the source of catechesis is to draw attention to the fact that catechesis must be impregnated and penetrated by the thought, the spirit and the outlook of the Bible and the Gospels through assiduous contact with the texts themselves."

"When you are sad, open the Scriptures and you will find the passage that will console you. Do the same in times of doubt and fear. During every uncertainty or anxiety, the saints went to this fount. God will guide and direct you!

"The Bible does not only teach us how to live well as individuals, nor does it only teach us about domestic virtues, or only about what refers to religion. It also teaches us about all that can be grouped under the heading of social virtues.

"The Bible teaches love among nations, love among the various social classes, the duties of owners toward employees and the duty of workers toward employers. It teaches justice and honesty in commerce and business, love for work, various forms of apostolate for the young, the elderly, the sick. It teaches the spiritual and corporal works of mercy.

"Would we ever have understood the meaning of humility, gentleness, patience, the bearing of wrongs, virginity, and fraternal charity spurred to the point of self-immolation if we had never read and meditated on the examples and lessons of our Lord?"
Rev. James Alberione, SSP, STD

Before Reading Sacred Scripture

O Jesus Christ, our Master, You are the Way and the Truth and the Life. Grant that we may learn the supereminent knowledge of Your charity in the spirit of St. Paul the Apostle and of the Catholic Church. Send Your Holy Spirit to teach us and remind us of what You preached.

Jesus Master, Way and Truth and Life, have mercy on us.

After Reading Sacred Scripture

Jesus, Divine Master, You have words of eternal life.
I believe, O Lord and *Truth,* but increase my faith.
I love You, O Lord and *Way,* with all my strength, because You have commanded us to observe Your commandments perfectly.

I pray to You, O Lord and *Life:* I adore You, I praise You, I beseech You, and I thank You for the gift of Sacred Scripture.

With Mary, I shall remember and preserve Your words in my mind, and I shall meditate on them in my heart.

Jesus Master, Way and Truth and Life, have mercy on us.

Introduction

GOD'S MESSAGE TO US

Despite all material achievement, many struggle today, as in the past, with vital problems. But by reading the Bible one can obtain divine help, for in Scripture we find God's living voice, His message regarding Himself, His infinite love for us, and His divine will concerning our life and destiny.

The Holy Bible contains the revelation of God, the message of salvation. Pope Leo XIII called it our heavenly Father's letter to us, which—transmitted through the sacred writers—guides God's children on their earthly pilgrimage.

In its *Dogmatic Constitution on Divine Revelation,* Vatican II states: "In His goodness and wisdom God chose to reveal Himself and to make known to us the hidden purpose of His will (cf. Eph. 1:9) by which through Christ, the Word made flesh, man might in the Holy Spirit have access to the Father and come to share in the divine nature (cf. Eph. 2:18; 2 Pt. 1:4).... By this revelation the deepest truth about God and the salvation of man shines out for our sake in Christ, who is both the Mediator and the fullness of all revelation" (n. 2).

The Bible, then, is truly the Word of God. We need this Word, for although God's existence and the immortality of the human soul can be known by human reason, the *total purpose* of our lives—the nature of our ultimate destiny—cannot be learned through experience or philosophy.

Someone might ask, however: "How can we be sure that the Judaeo-Christian Scriptures, as compared with the sacred writings of other religions, contain the pure, Divine Revelation?" This certitude may be reached in the following manner:

1) It can be proven that the Gospels—the key books of the Bible—are genuine, truthful historical documents. 2) As a result, the central message of the Gospels—Jesus' divinity—can be accepted, as well as 3) His institution of a Church, which He promised to be with until the end of time (cf. Mt. 28:20). 4) The next logical step is acceptance of the Church's declaration that the Scriptures, together with Sacred Tradition,° contain God's revelation to man in its fullness. (We can also acknowledge the Church's right to interpret Scripture for us in the name of Christ, under the guidance of the Holy Spirit, who leads her in the truth—cf. Jn. 16:13.)

This is how the authenticity and truthfulness of the Gospels can be established:

Ancient Christian and pagan sources show that the Gospels were written in the early years of Christianity. Some of the sources name the writers: Matthew, Mark, Luke and John. Moreover, much of the data in the Gospels has been confirmed by writings of that period and by archaeological discoveries of our own day.

As just stated, the evangelists (Gospel writers) have been identified as eyewitnesses or disciples of eyewitnesses of Jesus' teachings and miracles. And these men were writing for *other* eyewitnesses and *their* disciples. Thus, we can be sure that the evangelists wrote only what *all* the early Christians knew about Jesus: The communities of Christ's followers would not have permitted the diffusion of errors or falsifications.

We know, furthermore, that the Gospels could not have been falsified *later,* for the thousands of ancient manuscripts that have been found throughout the

---

°Tradition in this sense means the teachings of Jesus not recorded in the New Testament which were nonetheless transmitted to the Church through the word and example of the Apostles.

Mediterranean world differ only in the slightest details—such variations as would be expected in manuscripts that had been painstakingly copied by hand.

Declares Vatican II: "Holy Mother Church has firmly and with absolute constancy held, and continues to hold, that the four Gospels just named, whose historical character the Church unhesitatingly asserts, faithfully hand on what Jesus Christ, while living among men, really did and taught for their eternal salvation until the day He was taken up into heaven (cf. Acts 1:1). Indeed, after the ascension of the Lord, the Apostles handed on to their hearers what He had said and done. This they did with that clearer understanding which they enjoyed after they had been instructed by the glorious events of Christ's life and taught by the light of the Spirit of truth. The sacred authors wrote the four Gospels, selecting some things from the many which had been handed on by word of mouth or in writing, reducing some of them to a synthesis, explaining some things in view of the situation of their churches, and preserving the form of proclamation but always in such fashion that they told us the honest truth about Jesus. For their intention in writing was that either from their own memory and recollections, or from the witness of those who 'themselves from the beginning were eyewitnesses and ministers of the Word' we might know 'the truth' concerning those matters about which we have been instructed (cf. Lk. 1:2-4)" *(Dogmatic Constitution on Divine Revelation, n. 19)*.

SACRED SCRIPTURE AND SACRED TRADITION

Just as there can be only one all-perfect Being—only one God—so there can be only one system of truths about God and man—only one Revelation. As we have seen, this Revelation comes to us from Jesus Christ in the form of Scripture and Sacred Tradition—first, transmitted through His Apostles; now, through the Church.

The Bible itself tells us that some teachings of and about Jesus were passed on orally: "There are also many other things which Jesus did; were every one of them to be written, I suppose that the world itself could not contain the books that would be written" (Jn. 21:25). "Stand firm and hold to the traditions which you were taught by us, either by word of mouth or by letter" (2 Thes. 2:15).* "What you have heard from me before many witnesses entrust to faithful men who will be able to teach others also" (2 Tm. 2:2).*

And, just as the Bible refers to Sacred Tradition, so *it is through Tradition* that we know which Hebrew and Christian writings constitute the Bible. (The Bible itself does not contain a list of the inspired books!)

Declares Vatican II: "There exists a close connection and communication between Sacred Tradition and Sacred Scripture. For both of them, flowing from the same divine wellspring, in a certain way merge into a unity and tend toward the same end. For Sacred Scripture is the Word of God inasmuch as it is consigned to writing under the inspiration of the divine Spirit, while Sacred Tradition takes the Word of God, entrusted by Christ the Lord and the Holy Spirit to the Apostles, and hands it on to their successors in its full purity, so that led by the light of the Spirit of truth, they may in proclaiming it preserve this Word of God faithfully, explain it, and make it more widely known. Consequently it is not from Sacred Scripture alone that the Church draws her certainty about everything which has been revealed. Therefore both Sacred Tradition and Sacred Scripture are to be accepted and venerated with the same sense of loyalty and reverence.

"Sacred Tradition and Sacred Scripture form one sacred deposit of the Word of God, committed to the Church" *(Dogmatic Constitution on Divine Revelation,* nn. 9 and 10).

```
Sacred
Tradition
(passive)              (living)      Sacred Doctrine,
              Divine    active   →   taught by the
              Revelation→tradition   Magisterium, aided by
Sacred                               theologians
Scripture
```

THE BIBLE—A SACRED LIBRARY!

In Hebrew the Bible (Old Testament) is called the Writings. From this we derive our word Scriptures, which comes to us through the Latin. The word is plural because the Bible is made up of many parts, called books. The Greek word for Bible also acknowledged this structure: *ta Biblia* meant "the books." In Latin the form *Biblia* became singular: the Book. And, of course, the Bible is *the Book* par excellence, the world's best seller!

The Bible is composed of two parts, the Old Testament and the New Testament. "Testament" means both "covenant" (agreement between a lord and his vassal) and "last will." Both meanings shed light on these two major sections of the Bible. For example, the New Testament teaches us about the New Covenant; its benefits are the heritage Jesus willed to leave us through His death.

The Old Testament recounts the history of the chosen people, Israel, whom God made His own in order that they would witness to Him in the midst of a pagan world, which they would make ready for the coming of the Messiah. This history records faults and failings, to be sure, but these are not condoned; the pages of the Old Testament make clear the high moral code which Yahweh had given to His people.

The New Testament tells us of the birth, life, teachings, death and resurrection of Jesus Christ, the Son of God, as well as the early life and growth of His New Covenant people, the Church.

In making its canon—its official list—of the books of the Old Testament, the early Church followed the "Septuagint"—a Greek translation that we shall mention again later. The early Christians used the Septuagint to support their teaching about Jesus as the Messiah. St. Paul, too, used it in his preaching to the Gentile world. Millions of Eastern Christians use it even today in their liturgy, as they have done throughout the centuries.

The present-day Hebrew Scriptures do not contain all the books found in the Septuagint. A "Palestinian," or Jewish, canon was established around the end of the first century A.D. It contained only those books which were still available in the Hebrew language at that time. Other books, by then better known in Greek or in Aramaic (a common tongue related to Hebrew), were excluded by an extreme group of Pharisees, hostile to Roman domination and to everything which was not nationalistic. Although some of these books had originally been composed in Palestine in Aramaic or Hebrew, they were not accepted.

The Hebrew Scriptures, therefore, contain fewer books than the Catholic Old Testament. When Protestants began to make translations directly from the Hebrew, they dropped the same Old Testament books that had been excluded from the Jewish canon—namely, 1 and 2 Maccabees, Sirach, Wisdom, Baruch, Tobit, Judith, and portions of Esther and Daniel.

Regarding the New Testament, the Church accepted as Scripture those books which had a clear link with the Apostles, either directly or through close associates. Certain "gospels" originating in the second century were rejected. Other books originating from the first century were universally accepted only after they had been found to reflect the written and unwritten teaching of Christ.

By the year 400 (with the Councils of Hippo and Carthage in 393 and 397 A.D.), the Church had established the complete content of both Old and New Testaments. In the sixteenth century, the Council of Trent reaffirmed this list or *canon*.

"Canon" originally meant "measuring rod" and came to signify "rule" or "norm." Christianity early began to use this term to designate the written rule of faith: the Bible. "Canonical" means recognized as inspired and listed as such.

Trent declared canonical seven New Testament books which the first Protestants did not accept: Hebrews, James, 2 Peter, 2 and 3 John, Jude and Revelation. These seven books are called "deuterocanonical," as are the seven Old Testament books listed above. All the other books of the Bible are called "protocanonical." *Proto* means first; the protocanonical books had been accepted by Christians from the beginning. *Deutero* means second; the deuterocanonical books had been accepted more slowly by the early Church. But they *were* accepted on the basis of their use in instruction and in the liturgy, their doctrinal harmony with the rest of Scripture, and especially their link with the Apostles. Having been defined as inspired, they are as truly a part of Scripture as the protocanonical books. The Holy Spirit guides the Church.

Today Protestants, too, tend to accept the deuterocanonical books of the *New Testament*.

The books that the Catholic Church excluded from its canon in the early centuries are called *apocrypha*. Originally the word meant hidden or secret. Later it came to mean excluded from the Christian canon. There are many Old Testament apocrypha, some of them "apocalyptic," that is, treating of the approach of the end of the world, and a great struggle between good and evil. The New Testament apocrypha include many "gospels," the majority of them tainted with the heresy called gnosticism.

Our separated brethren use the term "apocrypha" in a different sense: They reserve it for our deuterocanonical books of the Old Testament, plus a few other writings. Some Protestant Bibles place these books in a separate section, preceded by the heading "Apocrypha," or even omit them entirely. In recent years, however, there has been a certain tendency toward accepting a broader canon that includes the deuterocanonical books.

Protestants often use the term *pseudepigrapha* ("false writings") for the books that we call apocrypha.

The Catholic Old Testament contains forty-five or forty-six books (depending on whether Lamentations is combined with Jeremiah); the Catholic New Testament, twenty-seven. One way of categorizing these books is as follows:

The Old Testament

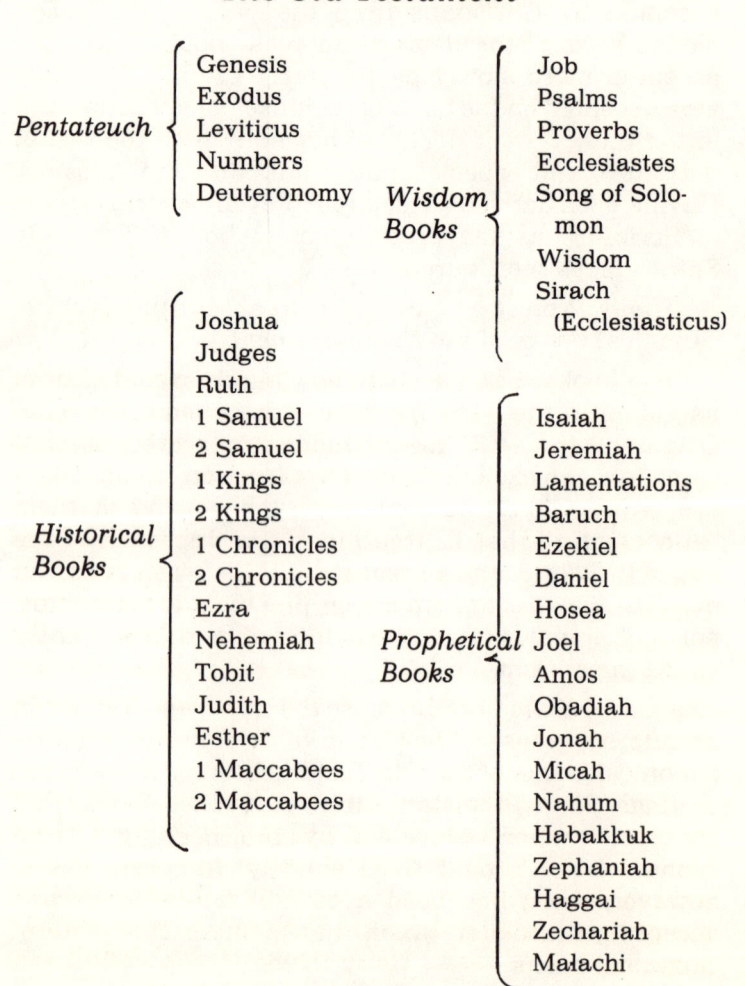

Pentateuch
- Genesis
- Exodus
- Leviticus
- Numbers
- Deuteronomy

Wisdom Books
- Job
- Psalms
- Proverbs
- Ecclesiastes
- Song of Solomon
- Wisdom
- Sirach (Ecclesiasticus)

Historical Books
- Joshua
- Judges
- Ruth
- 1 Samuel
- 2 Samuel
- 1 Kings
- 2 Kings
- 1 Chronicles
- 2 Chronicles
- Ezra
- Nehemiah
- Tobit
- Judith
- Esther
- 1 Maccabees
- 2 Maccabees

Prophetical Books
- Isaiah
- Jeremiah
- Lamentations
- Baruch
- Ezekiel
- Daniel
- Hosea
- Joel
- Amos
- Obadiah
- Jonah
- Micah
- Nahum
- Habakkuk
- Zephaniah
- Haggai
- Zechariah
- Malachi

The New Testament

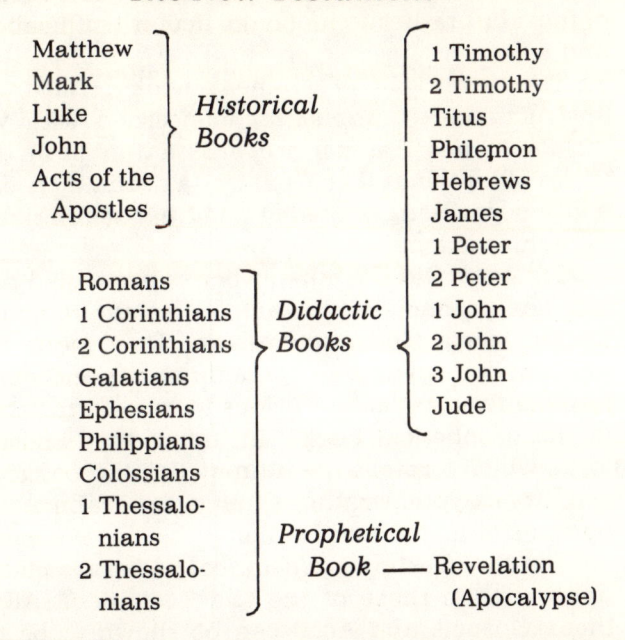

Historical Books:
- Matthew
- Mark
- Luke
- John
- Acts of the Apostles

Didactic Books:
- Romans
- 1 Corinthians
- 2 Corinthians
- Galatians
- Ephesians
- Philippians
- Colossians
- 1 Thessalonians
- 2 Thessalonians
- 1 Timothy
- 2 Timothy
- Titus
- Philemon
- Hebrews
- James
- 1 Peter
- 2 Peter
- 1 John
- 2 John
- 3 John
- Jude

Prophetical Book: Revelation (Apocalypse)

Even though this division has been made, the books within a given category may not all be similar. There are striking differences, particularly among the historical and wisdom books of the Old Testament.

If the Pentateuch is included, there are twenty-one Old Testament *historical* books. The Pentateuch, or Torah, comprises the five books that treat of pre-history, the call of Abraham, and the Israelites' journey to the promised land. The focus of these books is the covenant made at Mt. Sinai. Much of their content was transmitted orally for centuries.

Some of the histories, such as 2 Samuel, draw heavily on written records of the period. While most of the histories are truly historical, although not usually written the way we write history today, three books that are grouped among them are fictional, with or without some historical basis. These books (Tobit, Judith and

Esther) were not written to provide an objective record of facts but rather to teach particular truths about God and man.

The seven Old Testament books called *didactic* (instructional) or *sapiential* (concerned with wisdom) include hymns (Psalms), proverbs, a treatise on the emptiness of all things (Ecclesiastes), a dramatic poem (Job), a love poem (Song of Songs), and treatises on right living (Sirach, Wisdom).

Eighteen Old Testament books are called *prophetical*. The prophets—for example, Isaiah, Jeremiah and Ezekiel—were God's spokesmen. They made His will and plan known to their contemporaries and sometimes foretold future events. Various literary forms are found in the prophetical books, including the "apocalyptic" form, which foretells the ultimate triumph of good over evil. Apocalyptic writing is found, for example, in some portions of Isaiah and Daniel.

The New Testament *historical* books are much more uniform than those of the Old Testament. All five of them (Gospels and Acts) can be shown to be reliable historical documents, telling of the life of Jesus and the early years of the Church. Nonetheless, there are various literary forms within them.

Corresponding to the wisdom literature of the Old Testament are the *didactic,* or teaching, books of the New: twenty-one epistles (letters) written by the Apostles (and perhaps in some cases by their close associates). They contain valuable teachings about doctrine and Christian living.

There is only one *prophetical* book in the New Testament, and it is apocalyptic: the Book of Revelation or the Apocalypse. It was written to encourage Christians who were about to undergo persecution.

WHEN? WHERE? IN WHAT LANGUAGES?

The Bible was written over a period of about 1,300 years—probably from the era of the Israelites' journey out of Egypt until the last years of the Apostle St. John.

Most of the books of Scripture passed through a period —long or short—of oral transmission before they were committed to writing. Often, especially with regard to the Old Testament, various oral traditions and written fragments were fused in successive editings.

The Old Testament was written in Palestine, in neighboring lands such as Egypt, and in Mesopotamia. The New Testament was written in Palestine and in various other parts of the Greco-Roman world.

The original languages of the Bible were Hebrew, a related tongue called Aramaic, and Greek. Most of the Old Testament was written in Hebrew. Portions of Daniel, Ezra, Jeremiah, Esther and probably the Books of Tobit and Judith were written in Aramaic. Wisdom, 2 Maccabees and all the books of the New Testament were written in Greek. (An Aramaic Gospel of Matthew probably predated the longer Greek version but has been lost.)

TEXTS AND VERSIONS

The original writings of the inspired authors are no longer extant. The Bible has been transmitted to us through ancient copies called manuscripts and translations of them. The manuscripts are called *texts*, and the process of comparing them to try to verify the original wording is called *textual criticism*. Translations are called *versions*.

Two very famous versions of the Bible are the Septuagint and the Vulgate.

The *Septuagint* (meaning "seventy" and abbreviated with the Roman numerals LXX) was a translation of the Hebrew books of the Old Testament into Greek. Translated in Egypt during the third century B.C., the Septuagint was attributed to a large number of scholars—hence the name "seventy," which for the Hebrews meant a large number. This Greek Old Testament was widely used in the early Church.

The *Vulgate* was the Latin version prepared by Saint Jerome, who translated the Old Testament directly from the Hebrew and revised an existing Latin text of the New Testament. The Council of Trent approved an official edition of the Vulgate, which had been checked carefully for doctrinal orthodoxy (for during the centuries of hand-copying, slight variations had appeared in various copies). For many years, a translation of this, the Douay version, was the only authorized English version of the Bible. Now there are many approved translations, as a result of twentieth-century scholarship. Often these have been made from the original languages.

These translations are *not* efforts to give different interpretations. Each translation is an attempt to understand and to express the exact meaning of the sacred writer (and, therefore, of the Holy Spirit) in contemporary terminology that is both clear and appealing. Authorized translations are the work of dedicated scholars, expert in the languages and customs of the Bible world.

CHAPTERS AND VERSES

The Bible was not always divided into chapters and verses as it is today. The chapter division took place in the thirteenth century as a result of the work of Stephen Langton (later Archbishop of Canterbury). The division into verses was done in the mid-sixteenth century by a printer named Robert Estienne.

This division is helpful in assuring that no portion of the Bible will be lost. It is extremely useful for locating particular passages.

INSPIRATION AND INERRANCY

In its *Dogmatic Constitution on the Catholic Faith,* Vatican I describes Sacred Scripture as the collection of books which, "written under the inspiration of the Holy Spirit, has God as its Author, and has been entrusted to the Church as sacred and canonical" (chapter 2).

"Inspiration" with regard to Scripture has a very specific meaning. *Inspiration* was a direct, supernatural, charismatic influence on the mind, will and executive faculties of the human writer by which he mentally conceived, freely willed to write and actually did write—correctly—everything that God intended him to write, and nothing else, so that God is truly the Author of the sacred books.

Writes Leo XIII: "By supernatural power [the Holy Spirit] so moved and impelled them to write—He so assisted them when writing—that the things which He ordered, and those only, they, first, rightly understood, then willed faithfully to write down, and finally expressed in apt words and with infallible truth" (*On the Study of Sacred Scripture,* II D, 3a).

From inspiration derives *inerrancy.* The inerrancy of Scripture means that the sacred writings, as they were left by the human authors, were free from error.

States Vatican II: "Since everything asserted by the inspired authors or sacred writers must be held to be asserted by the Holy Spirit, it follows that the books of Scripture must be acknowledged as teaching solidly, faithfully and without error that truth which God wanted put into sacred writings for the sake of salvation" (*Dogmatic Constitution on Divine Revelation,* n. 11).

St. Augustine declares that any apparent errors in Scripture are to be ascribed to one or more of the following:

1) a faulty text (meaning a manuscript that contains an error made by a copyist)
2) an inaccurate translation
3) the reader's own lack of comprehension.

THE INTERPRETATION OF SCRIPTURE

Scripture itself tells us that ordinary individuals may wrongly interpret it:

"There are some things in them [Paul's letters] hard to understand, which the ignorant and unstable twist to their own destruction, as they do the other scriptures" (2 Pt. 3:16).*

Any written document needs some amount of interpretation, especially as times and circumstances change. The true interpretation of Scripture must be given by its principal Author, the Holy Spirit. He guides the teaching authority of the Church. Again, Scripture tells us: "You must understand this, that no prophecy of scripture is a matter of one's own interpretation, because no prophecy ever came by the impulse of man, but men moved by the Holy Spirit spoke from God" (2 Pt. 1:20-21).

Explains Vatican II: "The task of authentically interpreting the Word of God, whether written or handed on, has been entrusted exclusively to the living teaching office of the Church, whose authority is exercised in the name of Jesus Christ. This teaching office is not above the Word of God, but serves it. Teaching only what has been handed on, listening to it devoutly, guarding it scrupulously and explaining it faithfully in accord with a divine commission and with the help of the Holy Spirit, it draws from this one deposit of faith everything which it presents for belief as divinely revealed.

"It is clear, therefore, that Sacred Tradition, Sacred Scripture and the teaching authority of the Church, in accord with God's most wise design, are so linked and joined together that one cannot stand without the others" *(Dogmatic Constitution on Divine Revelation,* n. 10).

The Church, then, teaches us how Scripture is to be understood.

Scripture is to be understood literally, first of all. But this use of the word "literal" is somewhat different from our *normal* usage, where "literal" means "taken at face value." In Scripture studies, *the literal meaning is the sense intended by the sacred writer* (always—knowingly or otherwise—under divine inspiration). The literal meaning of a poetic or metaphorical passage of Scripture, therefore, is its *true meaning*, not simply the sense to be gleaned from a superficial reading. Genesis 1, for example, has been arranged in a particular pattern for easy memorization. The order of events is not to be taken at face value. The message (the literal meaning) is God's pre-existence, His transcendence, His power, His wisdom, His goodness, etc. Hence, the Church stresses the importance of knowing the literary form of a particular book or passage: By knowing the type of literature, one can unravel (or attempt to unravel) the sacred author's intended meaning—in other words, the primary meaning intended by God. *All of Scripture has a literal meaning*.

There is, however, at least one other sense of Scripture. This is the *spiritual or typical sense,* that is, *the deeper meaning a thing, person, place or event possesses because, according to the intention of God, it foreshadows something of the future*. This sense does not extend to all of Scripture, but only to certain persons, places, things or events. For example, Christ may be considered the "new Israel" and the "new Moses." Israel and Moses—besides having their own identities and histories—may be called *types* of Christ. They foreshadowed Him in some way. Likewise, the passage through the sea, an act of deliverance in the physical order, may also be considered a type of baptism, an act of deliverance in the spiritual order.

The sacred author may well have been unaware of the additional meaning his words conveyed. But Christ and His Apostles pointed it out. And this is the Church's guideline regarding the spiritual sense: It is best only to accept those "types" that the New Testament makes known to us, together with those hallowed by use in the early Church, for example, in her catechesis and liturgy.

To find a "spiritual sense" for everything is called *accommodation*. This was common in antiquity, especially in the East. Because accommodation is not inspired, its usefulness depends on its own intrinsic merits in each instance.

Many Catholic exegetes also speak of a "fuller" or "ampler" sense of Scripture. However, there is disagreement as to exactly what is meant by this "fuller" sense, and the major encyclicals on Scripture do not refer to it.

THE SCIENCE OF INTERPRETATION

Hermeneutics is the normative science of biblical interpretation and explanation. In practice, hermeneutics is called *exegesis.*

The principles of hermeneutics are derived from various disciplines and factors which have to be considered in explaining the Bible and its parts. Underlying all must be the truths and analogy of faith (see below). Then, in the light of these, all the following must be considered: the original language and the languages of translation, studied through philology and linguistics; the quality of the texts, studied through textual criticism; literary forms and genres, studied through literary and form criticism; cultural, historical, geographical and other conditions which influenced the writers, studied through archaeology, history, etc.; facts and truths of salvation history itself.

An exegete must never attempt to give a passage of Scripture a meaning *contrary* to the sense that the Church has declared it to have nor contrary to the "unanimous consent" (agreement of the great majority) of the Fathers of the Church, who were imbued with Sacred Tradition. These norms actually leave the Scripture scholar wide freedom, for he can *add* his own findings and insights to the above as long as he does not contradict them or the remainder of Scripture. The *"analogy of faith"* must be the guiding principle—meaning the harmony that always exists among all the Scriptures and between them and the teachings of the Church. God's truth is one.

Study of the *biblical languages* enables the exegete to read the words of Scripture in the original tongue rather than in translations (which may not always capture the full meaning of the words) and thus find greater depths of meaning and a wealth of relationships between texts.

Textual criticism endeavors to purify texts of Scripture from the omissions and changes of wording, generally slight, that gradually crept in during centuries of hand-copying, as well as from the explanations called "glosses" that had sometimes been inserted. By painstakingly comparing ancient manuscripts, scholars seek to make Scripture texts correspond as closely as possible to the original.

As a whole, the Bible cannot be understood correctly without awareness of the different *literary forms* found in various passages and books. Both Old and New Testaments contain diverse literary forms. This is especially true, however, of the Old Testament, where we find: epic, lyric and didactic poetry; drama; eyewitness accounts; epic history; pagan folklore adapted as a vehicle for monotheism; fictional tales; allegories; proverbs; maxims, and love stories.

The meaning of the biblical text can also be better understood and explained if an exegete can discover how the text was composed. Form and redaction criticism have endeavored to unravel the mysteries of such complex books as Genesis and Exodus, Matthew and Luke.

Form criticism attempts to reconstruct the history of the oral tradition behind certain of the sacred books. Regarding the Gospels, for example, form criticism postulates that these books were composed from many small oral units (of different literary forms) which were circulated separately in the Christian communities in response to particular needs. Form criticism is considered to contain some sound elements (for example, there *are* indications that the early Church cherished and related certain deeds or sayings of Jesus because of their own particular needs and problems), but it can be easily abused. Some form critics have thought and taught that the *content of the Gospels* was almost completely *created* by the early Christian community; in other words, that almost nothing in the Gospels has a real, historical basis in the life and teachings of Christ. This, of course, cannot be held. It undermines Christianity at its foundation. Vatican II refuted this type of thinking in the *Dogmatic Constitution on Divine Revelation* (no. 19), as we have seen.

Redaction criticism has yielded fruitful results. "Redaction" means "editing." In the case of the Gospels, the "editor" was the evangelist, who drew from oral and written sources in writing his account of the life of Jesus. Redaction criticism asks *why* a particular passage is included in Matthew but not in Luke, for example, or why Luke chose to arrange his material in one order while Matthew organized the same content differently. In other words, there is an endeavor to discover the sacred writer's (inspired) motivation—his theological purpose.

These kinds of criticism, when rightly used, can help an exegete to arrive better at the literal (true) meaning of a particular verse or passage.

Profane history, too, sheds great light on the biblical texts. Nineteenth and twentieth century archaeology has unearthed ancient buildings, artifacts and documents. Contemporary scientific techniques help in dating these. Many descriptions, many incidents, recounted in the Bible have now been fitted perfectly into their own times and places, whereas they had once been suspected of being legendary. All such findings—for instance, that of the literature of the Essenes near the Dead Sea—help scholars better to understand the background against which a particular book of the Bible must be viewed.

HOW SHOULD WE READ SCRIPTURE?

We should read Scripture with a prayerful spirit and readiness to put God's Word into practice.

Vatican II exhorts: "Prayer should accompany the reading of Sacred Scripture, so that God and man may talk together" *(Dogmatic Constitution on Divine Revelation,* n. 25).

Jesus Himself tells us how to respond to the inspired Word: "He taught them many things in parables, and in his teaching he said to them: 'Listen! A sower went out to sow. And as he sowed, some seed fell along the path, and the birds came and devoured it. Other seed fell on rocky ground, where it had not much soil, and immediately it sprang up, since it had no depth of soil; and when the sun rose it was scorched, and since it had no root it withered away. Other seed fell among thorns and the thorns grew up and choked it, and it yielded no grain. And other seeds fell into good soil and brought forth grain, growing up and increasing and yielding thirtyfold and sixtyfold and a hundredfold.' And he said, 'He who has ears to hear, let him hear.

" 'The sower sows the word. And these are the ones along the path, where the word is sown; when they hear, Satan immediately comes and takes away the word which is sown in them. And these in like manner are the ones sown upon rocky ground, who, when they hear the word, immediately receive it with joy; and they have no root in themselves, but endure for a while; then, when tribulation or persecution arises on account of the word, immediately they fall away. And others are the ones sown among thorns; they are those who hear the word, but the cares of the world, and the delight in riches, and the desire for other things, enter in and choke the word, and it proves unfruitful. But those that were sown upon the good soil are the ones who hear the word and accept it and bear fruit, thirtyfoid and sixtyfold and a hundredfold' " (Mk. 4:2-9; 14-20).

THE GEOGRAPHY OF THE HOLY LAND

In biblical times Palestine's position with regard to the great powers was significant. With a burning desert to the east and an almost harborless seacoast as its western boundary, the land of the Bible was situated on the great north-south road that connected the two horns of the fertile crescent—Egypt and Mesopotamia. In peacetime and in war, Palestine was a thoroughfare; through it caravans plodded and armies marched.

The topography of the land itself played an equally significant role in Palestine's history, for the lack of geographical unity contributed to the frequent religious and political diversity.

Even today such great diversity within an area so small (about the size of the state of Massachusetts) is striking.

First of all, Palestine is split into two unequal parts by the valley of the River Jordan. This great cleft is part of a geological fault—an earthquake zone—originating in the mountains north of the Holy Land and extending southward hundreds of miles into central Africa. Three lakes lie in this valley: the small Lake Huleh in the north, not mentioned in the Bible; the clear, fish-filled Sea of Galilee; and the warm, intensely salty Dead Sea to the south. Between the Sea of Galilee and the Dead Sea the River Jordan loops to and fro through dense forests, imprisoned by the walls of the great cleft. The valley descends to the lowest altitude in the world, 1,300 feet below sea level, at which point the Jordan empties into the Dead Sea. This large lake has no outlet, hence its name. No fish can live in these saltiest of waters. South of the Dead Sea the rift valley continues as the Arabah—a barren trough extending toward an arm of the Red Sea called the Gulf of Aqaba.

East of the rift valley, a high plateau merges with the Arabian Desert. The northern portion of this plateau was well wooded in biblical times; the southern had sparce vegetation.

The mountainous zone west of the rift valley is divided into three sections: the hill country of Judah, west of the Dead Sea; the central highlands of Samaria or Ephraim, separated from Judah by a belt of lower hills; and the fertile, fruitful highlands of Lower and Upper Galilee, north of Samaria. The Valley of Jezreel or Esdraelon separates Galilee from Samaria. These major highland zones are further cut by wadis—dry river beds which can become raging torrents in time of heavy rain.

To the west, each zone of hill country falls off to fuse with a fertile coastal plain: Asher in the north, beneath Mt. Carmel; Sharon, west of Samaria; and the Philistine Plain, west of the Judean Highlands. A belt of foothills, called the Shephelah (Shuh fay' lah), forms an intermediate zone between the mountains of Judah and the Philistine Plain. To the south of Judah lies the Negeb (Nay geb), the "dry land," transitional to the barren wastes of the Sinai Peninsula. The stark Judean hills that border on the rift valley constitute the Desert (or Wilderness) of Judah, whose cave-riddled cliffs are famous because of the Dead Sea scrolls discovered in them in the 1940's and '50's.

Thus, the Holy Land knows searing heat and pleasant coolness, aridity and fruitfulness. Its profusion of diverse regions and natural boundaries contributed to Israel's initial lack of unity and early rupture into two kingdoms, as well as to two opposing tendencies within the people themselves: the one toward the settled comfortable life, often coupled with worship of Canaanite agricultural deities, and the other toward the freer and more austere life of the seminomad, still faithful to Yahweh and to the desert experience that had made Israel His people. Even when monotheism triumphed in the final centuries B.C., these tendencies continued to manifest themselves, giving rise to the various sects and classes of people among whom the drama of the New Testament was to be played. The land of the Bible is a land of contradictions.

SOME HIGHLIGHTS OF PALESTINIAN HISTORY

Abraham — about 19th century B.C.
Israelites in Egypt — about 1700-1250 B.C.
exodus from Egypt — about 1240 B.C.
conquest of Canaan — about 1220-1200

period of Judges — about 1200-1030
David and Solomon — about 1010-931
schism; formation of the two kingdoms — 931
fall of northern kingdom to Assyria — 722-721
first deportation of Judahites to Babylon — 597
destruction of Jerusalem and Temple by
    Babylonians — 587
conquest of Babylon by Persia — 538
return of first exiles — 537
completion of second Temple — 515
conquest of Persians by Alexander the Great — 333
beginning of Maccabean revolt — 167
independence of Jewish state under Simon — 142
subjugation of Palestine by Romans — 63 B.C.
reign of Herod the Great — 37-4 B.C.
birth of Jesus Christ — about 6 B.C.°
public ministry of Jesus — probably 27-30 A.D.
death, resurrection and ascension of Jesus — 30 A.D.
conversion of Saul of Tarsus — around 36 A.D.
Council of Jerusalem — 49 or 50 A.D.
martyrdom of Peter and Paul — around 67
writing of the Gospels as we now have them
    — probably 60-100
Jewish revolt against Rome — 66
destruction of Temple by Romans — 70
Simon bar Kochba's revolt — 132
destruction of Jerusalem by Romans — 135
Byzantine rule over Palestine — 395-634
conquest of Palestine by Moslems — 634-636
capture of Jerusalem by crusaders — 1099
defeat of crusaders by Saladin (Moslem) — 1187
Turkish domination of Palestine — 1516-1918
British mandate over Palestine — 1922-1948
establishment of State of Israel — 1948

°The Christian calendar was to have been reckoned from Christ's birth but was based on a miscalculation.

The Old Testament

The Old Testament

From the Dogmatic Constitution on Divine Revelation, ch. 4

In carefully planning and preparing the salvation of the whole human race the God of infinite love, by a special dispensation, chose for Himself a people to whom He would entrust His promises. First He entered into a covenant with Abraham (cf. Gn. 15:18) and, through Moses, with the people of Israel (cf. Ex. 24:8). To this people which He had acquired for Himself, He so manifested Himself through words and deeds as the one true and living God that Israel came to know by experience the ways of God with men. Then too, when God Himself spoke to them through the mouth of the prophets, Israel daily gained a deeper and clearer understanding of His ways and made them more widely known among the nations (cf. Ps. 21:29; 95:1-3; Is. 2:1-5; Jer. 3:17). The plan of salvation foretold by the sacred authors, recounted and explained by them, is found as the true Word of God in the books of the Old Testament: these books, therefore, written under divine inspiration, remain permanently valuable. "For all that was written for our instruction, so that by steadfastness and the encouragement of the Scriptures we might have hope" (Rom. 15:4).

The principal purpose to which the plan of the old covenant was directed was to prepare for the coming of Christ, the Redeemer of all, and of the messianic kingdom, to announce this coming by prophecy (cf. Lk. 24:44; Jn. 5:39; 1 Pt. 1:10), and to indicate its meaning through various types (cf. 1 Cor. 10:12). Now the books of the Old Testament, in accordance with the state of mankind before the time of salvation established by Christ, reveal to all men the knowledge of God and of man and the ways in which God, just and merciful, deals with men. These books, though they also contain some things which are incomplete and temporary, nevertheless show us true divine pedagogy.[1] These same books, then, give expression to a lively sense of God, contain a store of sublime teachings about God, sound wisdom about human life, and a wonderful treasury of prayers, and in them the mystery of our salvation is present in a hidden way. Christians should receive them with reverence.

God, the Inspirer and Author of both Testaments, wisely arranged that the New Testament be hidden in the Old and the Old be made manifest in the New.[2] For, though Christ established the New Covenant in His blood (cf. Lk. 22:20; 1 Cor. 11:25), still the books of the Old Testament with all their parts, caught up into the proclamation of the Gospel,[3] acquire and show forth their full meaning in the New Testament (cf. Mt. 5:17; Lk. 24:27; Rom. 16:25-26; 2 Cor. 14:16) and in turn shed light on it and explain it.

---

1. Pius XI, encyclical *Mit Brennender Sorge*, March 14, 1937: *AAS* 29 (1937) p. 51. 2. Saint Augustine, *Quest. in Hept.* 2,73: PL 34, 623.   3. St. Irenaeus, *Against Heretics* III, 21,3: PG 7, 950; (Same as 25, 1: Harvey 2, p. 115). St. Cyril of Jerusalem, *Catech.* 4, 35; PG 33, 497. Theodore of Mopsuestia, *In Soph.* 1, 4-6: PG 66, 452D-453A.

The Pentateuch

Pentateuch is a Greek word which means "five books," the first five Books of the Bible: *Genesis, Exodus, Leviticus, Numbers,* and *Deuteronomy.* The Jewish people call them the *Torah* or the Law. They are, however, more than a body of legal doctrines. They give us the primitive history of mankind and the beginning of "salvation history," that is, the story of the formation of the People of God: Abraham and the patriarchs, Moses and the oppressed Hebrews in Egypt, the birth of Israel in the Sinai covenant, the journey to the threshold of the Promised Land, and the "discourses of Moses."

According to contemporary Pentateuchal study, this sacred history reveals a variety of styles and repetitions which make it impossible to ascribe the whole work to a single author. At the end of the nineteenth century the hypothesis which prevailed among the critics was that the Pentateuch is an amalgam of four documents written in different places and times: the *Yahwistic* (J), which uses the divine name *Yahweh* that was revealed to Moses; the *Elohistic* (E), which uses the common noun for God, *Elohim;* the *Deuteronomic* (D), characterized by the intense exhortatory style of Deuteronomy 5 through 11; and the *Priestly* (P), made up, for the most part, of genealogies and laws. According to this theory, the Pentateuch, in its present form, is the result of a careful and complex joining of the four sources by a compiler under the guidance of the Holy Spirit, probably after the Exile, around the late sixth or fifth century B.C. In substance, this four-source theory continues to be held, even though the origins of the Pentateuch are believed to be still more complex than this.

Why then, one might ask, have these five Books, or *Pentateuch,* been considered the "five Books of Moses" by the Judaeo-Christian tradition?—They have been considered such because of the great role Moses plays in them as the first and greatest prophet, and especially as lawgiver par excellence.

The fundamental characteristic of the whole Pentateuch is its religious meaning: "Planning to make known the way of heavenly salvation," says Vatican II, "God...from the start manifested Himself to our first parents. Then after their fall His promise of redemption aroused in them the hope of being saved (cf. Gn. 3:15) and from that time on He ceaselessly kept the human race in His care, to give eternal life to those who perseveringly do good in search of salvation (cf. Rom. 2:6-7). Then, at the time He had appointed, He called Abraham in order to make of him a great nation (cf. Gn. 12:2). Through the patriarchs, and after them through Moses and the prophets, He taught this people to acknowledge Him as the one living and true God, provident Father and just Judge, and to wait for the Savior promised by Him, and in this manner prepared the way for the Gospel down through the centuries" *(Dei Verbum,* no. 3).

From the great prophecies° of Genesis:
"I will put enmity between you and the woman,
and between your offspring and hers" (3:15),
up to the last one of Moses: "A prophet like me [the Messiah] will the Lord, your God, raise up for you from among your own kinsmen; to him you shall listen" (Dt. 18:15), the Pentateuch is a succession of promises that become always more clear—promises which transcend the future of the first People of God, Israel, and embrace the entire world. Jesus Christ is the fulfillment of the entire Old Testament, the new Legislator, the new, true Leader of the new People of God, which embraces all those who through faith become descendants of Abraham, *the man who believed* in God's promises.

° A prophecy is a message from God regarding the present or the future. It is uttered or written by a *prophet*—one who speaks for God.

The Pentateuch, therefore, must be read with our gaze turned to Christ and to the Christian life, for which it is a preparation.

STUDY QUESTIONS

1. *What does "Pentateuch" mean? What is its Jewish name?*
2. *Name the Books of the Pentateuch.*
3. *What, in general, does the Pentateuch contain?*
4. *Name what are considered to be the four main sources from which the Pentateuch was compiled.*
5. *Approximately when was the Pentateuch given its final form?*
6. *Why can these Books be called the "Books of Moses"?*

The Book of Genesis

Genesis is the first Book of the Bible. The title *Genesis* comes from the first word with which it starts: "In the beginning." Genesis is concerned with the origin of the world (Gn. 1:1; 2:4) and of the human race, and in particular with the Hebrew people who were chosen by God to be the instrument of His plan of salvation.

From the theological point of view the Book of Genesis is fundamental. In it are treated and divinely answered the tormenting questions of the existence of man and the world, life and death, happiness and suffering. Genesis contains fundamental dogmas of our Christian religion. In fact, in regard to its content, the first eleven chapters are the most important. They tell of the creation of the universe; of the special creation of man and woman in God's image and likeness; of the institution of marriage as the union of one man with one woman; of the fall and its consequences for our first parents and their posterity; of the reconciliation offered by God with the promise of a Redeemer for fallen mankind; of the increase of human wickedness, which culminated in the punishment of the flood; of the repopulation of the earth starting with Noah and his sons.

Against the new erroneous opinions regarding the authenticity of the facts and truths contained in these first eleven chapters of Genesis, Pius XII in his Encyclical *Humani Generis* wrote: "...The first eleven chapters of Genesis, although properly speaking not conforming to the historical method used by the best Greek and Latin writers or by competent authors of our time, do nevertheless pertain to history in a true sense.... If...the ancient sacred writers have taken anything from popular narrations (and this may be conceded), it must never be forgotten that they did so with the help of divine inspiration, through which they were rendered immune from any error in selecting and evaluating those documents.

"Therefore, whatever of the popular narrations have been inserted into the Sacred Scriptures must in no way be considered on a par with myths or other such things, which are more the product of an extravagant imagination than of that striving for truth and simplicity which in the Sacred Books, also of the Old Testament, is so apparent that our ancient sacred writers must be admitted to be clearly superior to the ancient profane writers" (nn. 38 and 39).

With chapter 12 the *history of the chosen people* begins with the call of Abraham, the man blessed by God for his faith and obedience. Abraham is to be a blessing for all nations through his offspring: Isaac, Jacob and Jacob's sons, of whom the Messiah, the Redeemer of mankind, would be born. Before dying, "Jacob called his sons and said: 'Gather around, that I may tell you what is to happen to you in days to come... You, Judah, shall your brothers praise....
The scepter shall never depart from Judah...,
While tribute is brought to him;
   and he receives the peoples' homage" (Gn. 49:8, 10). Here the messianic prophecy is explicit.

Frequent references to Genesis are found in the New Testament. A few examples of these are in the Letters of St. Paul. To the Romans Paul writes that sin came through Adam, but grace and life through Christ: "Through one man sin entered the world and with sin death, death thus coming to all men inasmuch as all sinned.... But the gift is not like the offense. For if by the offense of the one man all died, much more did the grace of God and the gracious gift of the one man, Jesus Christ, abound for all. The gift is entirely different from the sin committed by the one man. In the first case, the sentence followed upon one offense and brought condemnation, but in the second, the gift came after many offenses and brought acquittal. If death began its reign through one man because of his offense, much more shall those who receive the overflowing grace and gift of justice live and reign through the one man, Jesus Christ" (Rom. 5:12, 15-17). To the Galatians St. Paul points out Abraham's faith, to prove that justification comes through faith: "Because Scripture saw in advance that God's way of justifying the Gentiles would be through faith, it foretold this good news to Abraham: 'All nations shall be blessed in you' " (Gal. 3:8). In his first letter St. Peter also refers to Noah's ark as the symbol of the Church, by which humanity is saved from destruction through the waters of Baptism: "They had disobeyed as long ago as Noah's day, while God patiently waited until the ark was built. At that time, a few persons, eight in all, escaped in the ark through the water. You are now saved by a baptismal bath which corresponds to this exactly. This baptism is no removal of physical stain, but the pledge to God of an irreproachable conscience through the resurrection of Jesus Christ. He went to heaven and is at God's right hand, with angelic rulers and powers subjected to him" (1 Pt. 3:20-22).

We are now starting the reading of the Book of Genesis. We will not be looking for a scientific presentation, but we will pray instead to understand the purpose of the Old Testament as preparation for the New and to profit from the religious lessons it teaches: the goodness of all God's creation; the need to rest on the seventh day; the gratitude we owe God for having made us in His image and likeness; the divine plan in making marriage one and indissoluble; the punishment which will fall upon anyone who abuses the gift of freedom to offend God; the immense trust we should have in our Redeemer; the importance of offering sacrifices in gratitude to our Creator, and more.

May the Holy Spirit, the Inspirer of the Bible, grant us His special light, strength and warmth to meditate upon God's living Word and to live by it. Let us pray:

"Come, Holy Spirit, fill the hearts of your faithful and enkindle in them the fire of Your love. Send forth your Spirit and they shall be created—and You shall renew the face of the earth."

STUDY QUESTIONS

1. What does "Genesis" mean and with what in general is this book concerned?
2. State four key points taught in the first eleven chapters of Genesis.
3. What must we understand about any popular narratives of the ancient Near East that were incorporated into the Bible?
4. Sum up some of the New Testament references to the Book of Genesis.
5. Name the important religious lessons that the Book of Genesis teaches us.

The Book of Exodus

The second book of the Old Testament is called *Exodus,* a Greek word which means "departure" or "going out."

The first major theme of Exodus is, in fact, the miraculous deliverance of the descendants of Jacob from slavery in Egypt through the mediation of Moses (1:1—15:21).

The second major theme is the Sinaitic Covenant° (19:1—40:38), in which, through Moses, God made the Israelites°° His special people and gave them His Law. The center of God's Law was the Decalogue, or Ten Commandments, which are valid for all people and for all times. Besides the Ten Commandments the Law included many other rules concerning charity toward others, especially the poor, and numerous prescriptions governing Israel's worship. Through that Law the chosen people were to become a holy people in whom the promise of a Savior for all mankind would be fulfilled.

Between the two major themes runs a secondary one: the journey through the wilderness in which the

---

°The Sinaitic Covenant was an agreement made at Mt. Sinai in which Yahweh ("He Who Is"—the name under which God chose to reveal Himself) took the descendants of Abraham as His own particular people. The covenant was structured as an agreement between a lord and his subject: Yahweh would protect His people if they would serve Him by obeying His laws.

°°The name "Israelite" comes from "Israel," a name which God bestowed on Jacob through an angel (Gn. 32:29). Occasionally the Bible calls God's people "Hebrews." After the Exile they were frequently spoken of as "Jews," because the majority of those repatriated were of the tribe of Judah, whereas the term "Israel" had come to be associated with the other tribes as a group. The name of the Jewish religion as practiced after the Exile was Judaism.

Israelites are described as discouraged and quarreling (15:22—18:27), a journey to the mountain of God—Horeb, also called Sinai.

Between the prescriptions of the Law (chapters 32 through 34) an account is given of the defections of the people together with the tragic story of infidelity while Moses was up on Sinai—the worshiping of the golden calf—and of God's anger, of which later He relented because of Moses' imploring prayers and the renewal of the covenant.

Exodus is a very important book because, while Genesis gives Israel's ancestral origin, in Exodus the history of the chosen people begins. God remembers His covenant with Abraham, Isaac and Jacob. He forms their descendants into a unified group and enters with them into a divine covenant.

The Book of Exodus had great importance for the theology and life of Israel. In it the chosen people saw the promise of the continual assistance of God. This fact can be seen in the prophetic writing, where the prophets recall the powerful deeds of Yahweh, His saving deeds, which He will repeat against present enemies (cf. Is. 40-55).

References to Exodus are frequent in the Book of Psalms in the form of supplication, as in Psalm 77, and especially in hymns of thanksgiving and praise for all the wonders of God (Pss. 68, 99, 105, 114, 135, 136).

The New Testament, too, uses Exodus themes abundantly. Jesus, for example, is portrayed as the new Moses, who is to lead His new people out of the slavery of sin through the waters of Baptism.

In the Sermon on the Mount Jesus is clearly presented as the new Moses, who gives a new and perfect law, which is the fulfillment of the Mosaic moral law: "You have heard the commandment imposed on your forefathers.... What I say to you is..." (Mt. 5-7).

In the Gospel of St. John Jesus speaks about an imperishable food, better than the mysterious manna which rained down from heaven for the Jews during their nomadic desert life of forty years. Jesus says that He is the "bread of life" (Jn. 6:24-35).

The influence of Exodus can also be seen in St. Paul. In 2 Corinthians 3:1-18, for example, he compares the covenant of the Old Testament with the new and perfect Covenant of the New Testament, the Covenant of Christ which gives freedom and life through the Spirit.

In his moral exhortations to the Christians of Corinth, Paul warns them not to follow the example of the old people of God who disobeyed Yahweh. After having listed many of their wicked deeds and corresponding punishments, he concludes: "...The things that happened to them serve as an example" (1 Cor. 10:1-11).

The Church uses Exodus abundantly in the readings of the liturgy.

We, the new People of God, now embracing *people of every nation,* can consider the Book of Exodus very timely because it is intensely human. In it we are touched especially by the fact that over and above the weakness and fickleness of people stands the infinite patience and mercy of God, a God "slow to anger and rich in kindness and fidelity" (Ex. 34:6) toward whomever turns to Him in repentance and trust.

STUDY QUESTIONS

1. *What does "Exodus" mean?*
2. *What are the major themes of this book?*
3. *What place did this book hold for the chosen people in later years?*
4. *Sum up four references to Exodus made in the New Testament.*

The Book of Leviticus

The Book of Leviticus is the third book of the Bible. It is the liturgical° book par excellence of the Old Testament. Thus, its name *Leviticus* comes from its contents, a good part of which consists of sacrificial and ritual laws prescribed for the priests of the tribe of Levi. They were laws given by God to Moses on Mt. Sinai and later developed with the changing of conditions.

The main divisions of Leviticus are:
1. ritual of sacrifices (1:1—7:38)
2. ceremonial for priestly ordination (8:1—10:20)
3. laws regarding legal purity (11:1—16:34)
4. code of legal holiness (17:1—23:44)
5. various other laws (24:1—26)

A last chapter (chapter 27) lays down the conditions for the redeeming of votive offerings.°°

With the coming of Jesus Christ Leviticus lost much of its importance because its main purpose was to prepare the way for the redemptive sacrifice of Christ, the Man-God, who with His own sacrifice on the cross brought about universal and eternal redemption (cf. Heb. chapters 9 and 10).

Notwithstanding this, it is important to note how the laws of Leviticus stress that the whole purpose of living is the attainment of holiness. This is a demand that holds even for us, the new People of God. To remind us of this, the Church uses in the liturgy the following beautiful passage:

°Liturgical—having to do with the ceremonies of worship.
°°Votive offerings—offerings not established by law but freely vowed to God.

"The Lord said to Moses, 'Speak to the whole Israelite community and tell them: Be holy, for I, the Lord your God, am holy'" (Lv. 19:1-2). And: "You shall not bear hatred for your brother in your heart. Though you may have to reprove your fellow man, do not incur sin because of him. Take no revenge and cherish no grudge against your fellow countrymen. You shall love your neighbor as yourself. I am the Lord" (Lv. 19:17-18).

Here is God's instruction about being holy and charitable. But while in the Old Testament the neighbor was exclusively Israelite, in the New Testament Jesus declared brotherhood universal.

STUDY QUESTIONS

1. *Where does the name "Leviticus" come from?*
2. *What, in general, does this book treat?*
3. *What is the most important application of the teachings of Leviticus to our life today?*

The Book of Numbers

The Book of Numbers is the fourth book of the Bible. It derives its name from the account of two censuses of the Israelites, the first taken as their desert journey was beginning (chapter 1), and the other nearly forty years later (chapter 26).

The importance of the Book of Numbers, however, lies in its central theme, which is the story of what took place while the people of Israel were in the desert. Thus, *Numbers* links up with *Exodus*, because it starts where Exodus ends, that is, right after the ratification of the covenant at Mt. Sinai. It carries through a period of thirty-eight years to the eve of the entry into the Promised Land, Canaan.

As all biblical history, Numbers, too, is *religious history*, which does not furnish an account of all the events which took place during the wilderness wandering, as modern historians would do. Instead, this book records only those events which manifest divine, rather than human, activity.

Numbers is also linked with *Leviticus* because it contains further legislation, either supplementing the Sinaitic code, or preparing for the time when the people will have settled in Canaan.

Geographically speaking, the book of Numbers can be divided as follows:

1. Preparation for the departure from Sinai (1:1—10:10)

2. The journey from Sinai to the Plains of Moab (10:11—22:1)

3. On the Plains of Moab (22:2—36:13)

In Numbers the action of God is continually present through the various events of His people. He is a God who dwells among them; despite their constant grumbling they are the object of His steadfast love. Even when He has to punish them, God never totally abandons them. Regardless of their lack of appreciation for having been saved from the slavery of Egypt and having been made a free people, despite their recalcitrance, the Lord brings them to the Promised Land. How many times Moses has to plead with the Lord on their behalf and the Lord listens to the prayers of His faithful servant!

The Book of Numbers contains many religious values from which every reader can profit. The New Testament underlines some of these values. St. John, for example, recalls in his Gospel that Moses lifted up the serpent in the desert (Jn. 3:14-15). Referring to this Gospel passage, St. Augustine comments: "...as those who looked at the bronze serpent mounted on the pole recovered, so too those who look at Jesus lifted up on the cross will be free from their faults." Other verses in the New Testament that refer to Numbers are: 1 Corinthians 10:10; 2 Peter 2:15f.; Hebrews 3:12-19.

The Church, too, takes a beautiful prayer from Numbers and reads it in the liturgy every New Year's Day, to ask God to bless us during the year ahead. It is that same prayer which the priests of the Old Testament used when they blessed the people:

"The Lord bless you and keep you!
The Lord let his face shine upon you, and be gracious
   to you!
The Lord look upon you kindly and give you peace!"
   (Nm. 6:24-26)

STUDY QUESTIONS

1. *Why was the fourth book of the Bible given the name "Numbers"?*
2. *What, in general, is this book about?*
3. *Look up and summarize two New Testament references to Numbers.*

The Book of Deuteronomy

The Book of Deuteronomy is the fifth and last book of the Pentateuch. The name "Deuteronomy" means "second law." And such it can be considered, since it is an updated presentation of the Law of Moses, given as Moses' farewell address, applied to the new conditions of the people, now no longer nomadic. This book reflects not only the period of which it speaks but also a period hundreds of years later when loyalty to the covenant needed to be reawakened.

The events contained in Deuteronomy took place on the plains of Moab (Dt. 1:5), between the end of the wanderings in the desert (Dt. 1:3) and the crossing of the Jordan River (Jos. 4:19); a period of about forty days. There, at the threshold of the Promised Land, Moses spoke at length to God's People, offering them a new chance to enter into covenant with God and to be faithful to Him.

The special characteristic of Deuteronomy is its forceful oratorical style. The author of Deuteronomy is not satisfied with an ordinary exposition of laws, but he admonishes, animates, fills with fervor, threatens and makes promises.

Deuteronomy contains four eloquent discourses of Moses. They are the testament of this great leader and legislator, full of warmth and affection.

The first discourse (Dt. 1:1—4:43) is an historical review and exhortation. In it God's Providence is recalled and obedience and fidelity to Him are stressed.

The second and third discourses (4:44—26:19) constitute the central part of the book, an introduction to the Law, followed by the true deuteronomic code.°

The fourth discourse (Dt. 27:1—34:12) contains the final words of Moses; the call of Joshua; Moses' blessing upon the tribes; his death and burial.

Notwithstanding its character, essentially legal, Deuteronomy is a unique book, representing the apex of the Old Testament's religion.

The New Testament quotes it more than eighty times. Jesus Himself quoted passages of Deuteronomy in overcoming the threefold temptation of Satan in the desert (Mt. chapter 4; Dt. 6:13, 16; 8:3; 10:20), and in explaining to the lawyer the first and greatest commandment (Mt. 22:35-39; Dt. 6:4).

The Church uses passages from Deuteronomy in the readings of the liturgy several times during the year. One of these passages is that which can be considered the keynote of the Book of Deuteronomy: The Lord alone is God; we must love Him with an undivided heart. Here are the oratorical words of Moses:

"That you may fear the Lord your God, you and your son and your son's son, by keeping all his statutes and his commandments, which I command you, all the days of your life; and that your days may be prolonged. Hear therefore, O Israel, and be careful to do them; that it may go well with you, and that you may multiply greatly, as the Lord, the God of your fathers, has promised you, in a land flowing with milk and honey.

"Hear, O Israel: The Lord our God is one Lord; and you shall love the Lord your God with all your heart, and with all your soul, and with all your might. And these words which I command you this day shall be upon your heart" (Dt. 6:2-6).*

In Deuteronomy the reader breathes an atmosphere of immense love for God, who is all good and merciful, and of great benevolence toward neighbor. True love

---

°The deuteronomic code (Dt. 12:1—26:19) contained various kinds of laws covering every aspect of national life.

of God, in fact, cannot be limited to accomplishing religious duties, but is to be extended also to one's domestic and social life.

STUDY QUESTIONS

1. *What does Deuteronomy mean and why was this book so named?*
2. *Of what does this book consist?*
3. *What, in your opinion, is the special usefulness of this book for the Christian?*

The Book of Joshua

In the Bible the Book of Joshua follows the "Five Books of Moses." It is the first of a series of books, introduced by the Book of Deuteronomy, a *Deuteronomic History* and extends all the way through Judges, Samuel and Kings. This is called "salvation history," drawn up in keeping with Deuteronomy 32:7.

"Think back on the days of old,
   reflect on the years of age upon age.
Ask your father and he will inform you,
   ask your elders and they will tell you...."

This book takes its name from its great hero: *Joshua*. Joshua had been the right hand of Moses, and Moses himself commissioned him as his successor according to the will of God: "Moses said to the Lord, 'Let the Lord, the God of the spirits of all flesh, appoint a man over the congregation, who shall go out before them and come in before them, who shall lead them out and bring them in; that the congregation of the Lord may not be as sheep which have no shepherd.' And the Lord said to Moses, 'Take Joshua the son of Nun, a man in whom is the spirit, and lay your hand upon him; cause him to stand before Eleazar the priest and all the congregation, and you shall commission him in their sight. You shall invest him with some of your authority, that all the congregation of the people of Israel may obey'" (Nm. 27:15-20).*

Joshua was not a legislator as was Moses, but rather the great conquerer. Under his leadership the conquest of the Promised Land took place.

The facts narrated in this book, even though written in an epic style and idealized, actually took place —sometime about the end of the 13th century B.C.

According to scholars, the Book of Joshua was produced by a group of editors who compiled it from traditional material some six centuries after the conquest. It may be divided as follows:
1. Conquest of Canaan (1:1—12:24)
2. Division of the land among the tribes (13:1—21:45)
3. Return of the Transjordan tribes and Joshua's farewell (22:1—24:33)

The purpose of this book is a religious one: to show God's fidelity in giving the Israelites the land He had promised them as an inheritance (Gn. 15:18ff.; Jos. 1:2ff.; 21:41ff.; 23:14ff.). "Now acknowledge with your whole heart and soul," states Joshua in his final plea to the people, "that not one of all the promises the Lord, your God, made to you has remained unfulfilled" (Jos. 23:14).

The climax of the book may be considered the solemn revival of the Covenant with Yahweh at Shechem (in central Palestine), in accord with the command given by Moses before his death (Dt. 11:29; 27:2-26): "Later Joshua built an altar to the Lord.... On this altar they offered holocausts....° Then were read aloud all the words of the law, the blessings and the curses, exactly as written in the book of the law..." (Jos. 8:30-35).

This momentous pact also welded the tribes together and was the only guarantee of political unity until the monarchy was established.

Before Joshua died, he again reminded the people of the divine goodness and again urged them to remain faithful to Yahweh by keeping His Law. Only on this condition would they prosper (Dt. 28 and Jos. 24).

The name *Joshua* means "God saves." Through the waters of the Jordan, Joshua led God's people to the Promised Land. The Fathers of the Church saw in him a foreshadowing of Jesus (whose name is the Greek form of Joshua) who leads His people, through the waters of Baptism, into God's kingdom.

°Holocausts—offerings entirely consumed by fire.

STUDY QUESTIONS

1. Who was Joshua and what did he accomplish?
2. What is the purpose of the Book of Joshua?
3. What is the climax of the book? Why was this event important?
4. How is Joshua himself considered a foreshadowing ("type") of Jesus?

The Book of Judges

The Book of *Judges* presents us with twelve heroes of Israel: six of them, along with Deborah, called "major judges," because the book gives more information about them; and the other six called "minor judges," because they were generally local and unimportant, and less information is given about them. The major judges were: Othniel, Ehud, Deborah and Barak, Gideon, Jephthah, and Samson.

The title "judges" does not mean magistrates or administrators of justice, but charismatic heroes —*military leaders* raised up by God in time of need. They exercised their authority over one or more tribes, but never over the entire nation. Regardless of which tribe each came from, or how different their temperaments were, their vocation was the same: They were sent by God to save the Israelites in time of danger. While, in general, they were rough and even brutal (here we are far from the teachings of the Gospel), yet they displayed remarkable faith in Yahweh, were completely committed to Him and attributed their victories only to Him.

According to modern scholars, the period of the judges extends from the entry of the Israelites into the Promised Land to the beginning of the reign of King David, sometime before 1000 B.C. The main enemies of Israel during this long and troubled period were the Canaanites, the Moabites, the Amorites, the Midianites, and, above all, the Philistines.

It is believed that the Book of Judges, too, as the preceding Book of Joshua, was compiled from different sources, most of them very ancient. An editor or editors gathered the various accounts into a remarkable unity, so that the moral theme of the book reflects clearly that *fidelity to God brings blessing; infidelity to Him means punishment and misery.*

But even the Book of Judges shows an all-merciful God: Any time His people repent, God immediately comes to their help by inspiring a judge, who liberates them from their enemies in the name of Yahweh (cf. Jgs. 2:10-23). Throughout the entire book, the stress is on this fourfold cycle: *sin, punishment, repentance, deliverance.*

The division of the book is as follows:

1. Palestine after the death of Joshua (1:1—3:6)
2. Stories of the judges (3:7—16:31)
3. The tribes of Dan and Benjamin in the days of the judges (17:1—21:25)

The author of the Letter to the Hebrews includes the judges among the great people of the Old Testament, because by faith they worked wonders (cf. Heb. 11:32-34). He tells us to take inspiration from them: "Therefore, since we for our part are surrounded by this cloud of witnesses, let us lay aside every encumbrance of sin which clings to us and persevere in running the race which lies ahead; let us keep our eyes fixed on Jesus, who inspires and perfects our faith" (Heb. 12:1-2).

STUDY QUESTIONS

1. *What did the judges do?*
2. *When was the period of the judges?*
3. *What is the moral theme of the Book of Judges?*

The Book of Ruth

The Book of Ruth is the very delicate and edifying story of a Moabite woman. After the death of her husband, who had come from Bethlehem with his parents to settle in Moab, Ruth refused to leave her mother-in-law, Naomi:

"Do not ask me to abandon or forsake you!" Ruth replied to the plea of Naomi, when she urged her to go "back to her people and her god," "for wherever you go I will go..., your people shall be my people, and your God my God. Wherever you die I will die" (Ru. 1:15-17).

So Ruth chose Yahweh's territory, embraced His religion and entrusted herself entirely to His protection.

Soon after, Boaz, a prominent relative of Naomi's deceased husband, married Ruth.

Thus the Lord rewarded Ruth's fidelity and filial piety! She, a foreigner, became the great-grandmother of David, and through him, an ancestress of Christ (Ru. 4:21-22).

David, the great king of Israel, thus had in his veins foreign Moabitic blood. This foreshadowed the universality of salvation which Jesus, of the family of David, was to bring to all races.

In the Bible Ruth's idyllic episode is placed after the Book of Judges, because it occurred during their times (Ru. 1:1), and before the Books of Samuel, because it introduces us to King David's ancestors. The author is not known, and the date of the book's writing is still disputed, but there is no doubt about its historical background.

The Hebrew people used to read this short masterpiece once a year, during the feast of Pentecost. They liked it because of its rich symbolism and especially because of its connection with King David.

The lessons of the Book of Ruth are as valuable today as they were at the time they were written. With this delicate story God also teaches us that He makes no distinction of race, and that He rewards good, no matter who does it (Acts 10:34-48; cf. Acts 17:29; Gal. 3:28; Rom. 3:29; 1 Cor. 12:13; Col. 3:11).

STUDY QUESTIONS

1. Who was Ruth and why was she important in the history of salvation?
2. What are some of the lessons of the Book of Ruth?

The First and Second Books of Samuel

In the Hebrew Bible the two Books of Samuel composed one single work called "Samuel." The division into two books was made by the Greek translators, who also grouped them with the Books of Kings and gave all of them one title: "the Four Books of Kingdoms," since they relate the history of the monarchy. Later St. Jerome in the Vulgate called them "the Books of Kings." In modern times most translations have gone back to the original Hebrew title "Samuel," but have kept the division into two books, calling them 1st and 2nd Samuel.

They cover a period of about a century, describing the closing of the time of the judges, the beginning and the establishment of the monarchy with Saul as first king, and the splendid reign of David. They are historical books, but, as the other historical books of the Bible, they do not give a complete and systematic account of everything that happened during that period. The editor, inspired by God, recorded only those events which were related to *salvation history*. In his work of editing from the ancient traditions he also respected the different viewpoints. This can be seen in the accounts of the appointment of Saul as king, the reasons for his downfall, his relationship with David, and more.

The two Books of Samuel can be divided as follows:
First Book:

1. History of the last judges, Eli and Samuel (1 Sm. 1:1—7:17)

2. Establishment of the monarchy in Israel (1 Sm. 8:1—12:25)

3. Saul and David (1 Sm. 13:1—2 Sm. 2:7)
Second Book:
4. The reign of David (2 Sm. 2:8—20:26)
5. Some appendices (2 Sm. 21:1—24:25).

The principle figures with which they deal are: Samuel, Saul and David.

Samuel is described as the last of the judges. He successfully exhorted his countrymen to fight the Philistines and was also a prophet esteemed by all, who anointed the king (1 Sm. chapters 1 to 7).

Saul, too, started as a judge, but when the Philistines were threatening the very existence of Israel, all the tribes invested him with a wider and lasting authority. Thus monarchical government began. From then on God exercised His power over His people through a human ruler.

Saul reigned for twenty years. At first he proved to be very successful because of his military victories (1 Sm. 11:14-15), but soon he disappointed Yahweh by his disobedience. God then withdrew His charismatic gifts from Saul and bestowed His favor on David (1 Sm. 15:10-35). To be thought over are the words of the prophet to the strong-headed king:

"Obedience is better than sacrifice...
Because you have rejected the command of the Lord,
   he, too, has rejected you as ruler" (1 Sm. 15:22-23).

Particularly interesting is the story of the reign of David, narrated in the second book. David reigned for forty years (2 Sm. 5:4-5): His was the ideal reign, and never before or after was there a king like him!

David was a great military leader and a resourceful administrator. Above all, he was loyal to Yahweh. Under him the Philistines were driven to their own frontiers once and for always; the unity of all the tribes of Israel reached its peak (even though they never amalgamated); the city of Jerusalem was captured from the Jebusites and made the political and religious capital of the kingdom; the Ark of the Covenant was brought there.

Yet, there is a well-known disgraceful episode in David's life: his sin of adultery with Bathsheba and his conspiracy to kill her husband Uriah in order to marry her. Nathan the prophet delivered Yahweh's stern rebuke to David for this crime. David sorrowfully admitted his sin and did penance for it: "I have sinned against the Lord," he said. Then God, who never despises a humble and contrite heart, answered him through Nathan: "The Lord on his part has forgiven your sin; you shall not die" (cf. 2 Sm. 11-12).

What makes the Books of Samuel especially important is a famous messianic prophecy: The time is around 1000 B.C.; the place is Jerusalem. King David wants to build a house or Temple to the Lord. The prophet Nathan instead brings God's promise to build *David* a house—a royal kingdom to last forever:

"...The Lord also reveals to you," said Nathan, "that he will establish a house for you.... Your house and your kingdom shall endure forever before me; your throne shall stand firm forever" (2 Sm. 7:11-17). From David's time on, therefore, the messianic ideal was always kept alive, because, as the Lord revealed, it was from David's dynasty that Christ, the promised Messiah, was to come. His kingdom would last forever. After His coming, in fact, when the people saluted Him as "Son of David," they were acknowledging Him as Messiah:

"Blessed is he who comes in the name of the Lord!
Blessed is the reign of our father David to come!"
(Mk. 11:9-10)

The New Testament refers three times to Nathan's prophecy: Acts 2:30; 2 Corinthians 6:18; Hebrews 1:5.

The Church, too, in the Liturgy of the Word, presents us with excerpts from the Books of Samuel, because these tell us how God prepared for the coming of Jesus Christ, the Messiah, our Savior, our Master, our King.

STUDY QUESTIONS

1. What period do the Books of Samuel cover?
2. Who was Samuel?
3. Who was Saul?
4. What were some of David's achievements?
5. How did the concept of a messianic king originate?

The First and Second Books of Kings

The two Books of Kings (originally a single, historical work) immediately follow the Books of Samuel and are a continuation of them. They embrace the latter part of the royal period of Israelite history, from the death of David (around 970 B.C.) to the destruction of Jerusalem and the deportation of the people by Nebuchadnezzar in 587 B.C.

These books begin with a description of the last days and death of David and the inauguration of Solomon, third and last king of the twelve tribes of Israel (1 Kgs. 1-2).

Then they give an account of the splendid reign of Solomon (1 Kgs. 1-12): his unsurpassed wisdom, his great power, his riches, and the magnificence of his buildings, particularly the Temple of Jerusalem, erected on the site designated by Yahweh for His worship.

Parallel histories of Israel in the north and of Judah in the south follow (1 Kgs. 12—2 Kgs. 17), together with accounts of the fall of the Kingdom of Israel in 721 and that of the Kingdom of Judah in 587.

Midway in his account the editor incorporates a lengthy selection from the stories of the prophets Elijah (1 Kgs. 17—2 Kgs. 1) and of his successor Elisha (2 Kgs. 2-13). These two great prophets were sent by God to oppose the ever-increasing idolatry; this was a very hard mission indeed, and they accomplished it—with God's help—through lives of virtue, through the working of miracles, and at the cost of great persecution.

Among the sources used by the editor, three are explicitly mentioned in the books themselves: a History of Solomon, the Annals of the Kings of Israel and the Annals of the Kings of Judah.

The biblical author, however, did not write history as history; he selected only those episodes which would support his religious purpose. He went back over four hundred years of the nation's history, to explain that the catastrophe which had overtaken the two kingdoms had been brought about by the kings' and the people's infidelity to the covenant and to the Temple. God's promises of help and protection were conditional (1 Kgs. 11; 2 Kgs. 17). He treated each of the two kingdoms individually in its religious aspect and passed judgment on each king. All the kings of Israel were condemned. Only eight of the kings of Judah were praised for their fidelity to Yahweh, but six of them with the restriction: "the high places were not destroyed." Only two, Hezekiah and Josiah, were unreservedly approved. Both of these kings carried out sweeping reforms. In fact, Josiah repaired the Temple, destroyed all the pagan shrines, centralized the worship of Yahweh in Jerusalem again, and brought about reforms in accord with the contents of the Book of the Law just rediscovered (2 Kgs. 22, 23).

Before concluding the book, the author wishes to revive in his repentant people the messianic promise about the perpetuity of David's dynasty, a promise which had never been annulled, and which Yahweh would fulfill notwithstanding all things to the contrary. Thus, we read that a mysterious change of heart takes place in the king of Babylon, the successor of Nebuchadnezzar. In the inaugural year of his own reign he releases from prison Jehoiachin, the Davidic king in exile in Babylon for already thirty-seven years. The king of Babylon "spoke kindly to him [the king of Judah] and gave him a throne higher than that of the other kings who were with him in Babylon" (2 Kgs 25:27-30). Here it is: the dynasty of David has not ended. God's *messianic promise,* as all His promises, will be fulfilled!

STUDY QUESTIONS

1. *What period is covered by the Books of Kings?*
2. *What purpose did the sacred author have in mind as he wrote this history?*
3. *Name some of the "heroes" of these books.*
4. *How does 2 Kings end?*

The First and Second Books of Chronicles

The two Books of Chronicles (originally a single book) came to us with two different titles: *Paraleipomena* or "the things left out" (from the Books of Kings), and *Chronicles* or "things of the day."

The first title—Paraleipomena—is from the Greek Septuagint, adopted also by St. Jerome in his Vulgate. However, this title could be misleading, because even though the Books of Chronicles deal more or less with the same period as the Books of Kings, yet they are not a supplement of them. They treat history from a different point of view and their purpose also is different. The purpose of the Books of Kings is to point out that the real cause of the fall of the kingdoms of Israel and Judah was the failure of the kings and of the people to observe God's Law. On the contrary, the aim of the author of the Books of Chronicles is to offer his contemporaries a lesson from past history in order to bring them to an awareness of their call as God's people and to encourage them, if they want to survive and prosper, to be faithful to God, by obeying His Law and by offering Him a true worship in the place in which He has chosen to dwell, the Temple of Jerusalem. The author points out to his countrymen the sources of their unfailing hope: the Davidic dynasty from which the Messiah will come, and their Temple (1 Chr. 28:4; 2 Chr. 7:12; 12:13).

The second title—Chronicles—is the translation of the Hebrew title: "Dibre Hayyamim" which literally means: "things of the day," that is: "the events of the past." This title seems more appropriate, because the Books of Chronicles (meaning *Annals*) present the largest religious historical view of the history of Israel: from

Adam to the return from the Exile, a history continued in the Books of Ezra and Nehemiah, which are probably by the same author. For this reason St. Jerome said that these books might well be called: "The Chronicle of the Whole of Sacred History."

The unknown author, here called *the Chronicler,* very probably was a Jerusalem Levite of the post-exilic period (probably living in the late 5th century to early 4th century B.C.). He wrote after the time of Ezra and Nehemiah, in a period when Israel was still under Persian rule politically, but was allowed to have Jewish religious leaders who governed according to the Law of Moses. The Temple, too, with its beautiful ceremonies, had again become the true center of the national life.

As sources the Chronicler used the canonical Books of *Genesis* and *Numbers* for the genealogies and *Samuel* and *Kings* for much of the rest. Many other works were also cited by him, but these are no longer in existence. Since, however, he sometimes used this material with variance from the sources, rather freely adding, subtracting, and selecting to fit his purpose, older commentaries doubted the historicity of the Books of Chronicles. But recent archaeological discoveries and historical investigations show the general trustworthiness of the author.

The fact is that the Chronicler is not an historian. He is a theologian, and his books are a theological interpretation of historical events. He is also a reformer, and an optimistic one. He reflects on Israel's long history.... The royalty had been a failure, but he still profoundly trusts in God's promises to the family of David, and with this in mind he gives a picture of a future ideal kingdom.

In the first book he summarizes the genealogical tables from Adam to the beginning of David's reign—chiefly those concerned with the tribe of Judah, the ancestors of David, the Levites and the population of Jerusalem (1 Chr. 1-9).

In chapter 10 of the first book, the Chronicler introduces the history of his hero, David, and carries it through the remainder of the book (1 Chr. 10-29). One can immediately see that the David of Chronicles is not the same as the David of the Second Book of Samuel. The Chronicler gives his readers a *religious* king. He leaves behind David's faults, briefly recalls some of his victories, gives prominence to the messianic prophecy of Nathan (1 Chr. 17), and lists especially the king's religious activities: the transportation of the Ark to Jerusalem (1 Chr. 15); the organization of worship, with the foundation of the Levites (1 Chr. 16); the long and detailed preparation for the construction of the Temple according to the plan given him by God Himself (1 Chr. 26:19); the organization of its service (1 Chr. 22-29); and finally the king's beautiful prayer exalting God's sovereignty and the mystery of His goodness.

In the second book the Chronicler starts with the account of the reign of Solomon, to which he dedicates nine chapters (2 Chr. 1-9). Solomon too is seen in an ideal way, second only to David. Therefore, his sins are not mentioned (1 Kgs. 11), but stress is placed on: his building of the Temple according to the plan passed on to him by his father David (1 Chr. 28:11; 2 Chr. 2-4); the splendor of the Temple, the dedication ceremonies, the magnificence of the liturgy (2 Chr. 5); the long and universal prayer of Solomon in which he recalls the favors shown to the house of David (2 Chr. 6:1-17); and finally, God's promises to Solomon (2 Chr. 7:12-22), accompanied, however, by a warning that infidelity will be followed by disaster.

After the splitting of the kingdom, following Solomon's death, the Chronicler is concerned only with the kingdom of Judah and with the Davidic dynasty. In his opinion the northern kingdom of Israel, having separated from Judah, has prevented itself from sharing in the divine messianic promises (2 Chr. 10-36). Judah's kings are judged individually according to their attitude toward the Temple and its cult. Particular importance is given to the two great reformers: Hezekiah (2 Chr. 28-32) and Josiah (2 Chr. 33-35).

The last years of the kingdom of Judah are covered very briefly. After Josiah, only evil kings sat on the throne. Thus the whole people, leaders and priests included, who mocked at the warning given by God through His prophets, were carried into Exile, and Jerusalem and the Temple were destroyed. The Chronicler writes: "Now Judah had been carried in captivity to Babylon because of its rebellion" (1 Chr. 9:1). Notwithstanding all this, the inspired author ends his book with a prospect of redemption. The Exile will end, and God will stir up Cyrus the Persian to rebuild the Temple at Jerusalem (2 Chr. 36). "In the first year of Cyrus, king of Persia," the author writes, "in order to fulfill the word of the Lord spoken by Jeremiah, the Lord inspired King Cyrus of Persia to issue this proclamation throughout his kingdom, both by word of mouth and in writing: 'Thus says Cyrus, king of Persia: All the kingdoms of the earth the Lord, the God of heaven, has given to me, and he has also charged me to build him a house in Jerusalem, which is in Judah. Whoever, therefore, among you belong to any part of his people, let him go up, and may his God be with him!'" (2 Chr. 36:22-23)

The Chronicler's supreme interest is the Temple and the splendor of its worship. His ideal is to gather the chosen people, all the twelve tribes, into *one* community united in the worship of the one, true God at the Temple of Jerusalem, and living in the spirit of David, so that God could continue to bestow His blessings upon them and fulfill His promises. This is also the way that Saint Peter sees us, the new People of God, a people giving primacy to the things of the spirit: "You, however, are," St. Peter writes to the first Christians, " 'a chosen race, a royal priesthood, a holy nation, a people he [God] claims for his own to proclaim the glorious works' of the One who called you from darkness into his marvelous light. Once you were no people, but now you are God's people; once there was no mercy for you, but now you have found mercy" (1 Pt. 2:9-11).

STUDY QUESTIONS

1. Why is "Paraleipomena" a less suitable title for these books than "Chronicles"?
2. What is the main emphasis of these books?
3. Around when are the Books of Chronicles believed to have been written?
4. How does the Chronicler treat David and Solomon? How does he treat the kingdom of Israel?
5. How do the Books of Chronicles end?
6. What is the Chronicler's aim?

The Books of Ezra and Nehemiah

Scholars generally agree that the Books of Ezra and Nehemiah are a continuation of the Books of Chronicles, with which they form a unified historical work. They also believe that the author is the same: the Chronicler. To some extent this belief is supported by the fact that the last few verses of 2 Chronicles (36:22-23) are repeated at the beginning of Ezra (1:1-3).

The Hebrew Bible and the Septuagint° considered Ezra and Nehemiah as a single book, under the name "Book of Ezra." It was only in the first centuries of Christianity that it was divided. Thus, in the Latin Vulgate we have two books under the titles "I and II Ezra." I Ezra corresponds to our present Book of Nehemiah.

These books are important because they are almost the only source for the history of Israel as a province of the Persian Empire (538 B.C.—331 B.C.).

In Ezra-Nehemiah the author narrates the great work done by these two pioneers for the moral, religious and material Jewish restoration after the Exile. He seems to describe, as present and real, that ideal picture which he had traced in the previous Books of Chronicles, namely: the small community which had returned to the Promised Land now united in the Temple, joined in the restored ancient liturgy, faithful in the observance of the Law of Moses, and living as a community governed by men of their own race.

°The Septuagint was a Greek translation of the Hebrew Bible made at Alexandria, Egypt, in the 3rd century B.C. The early Church made wide use of this Greek version.

Having kept silent regarding the fifty years of exile, the Chronicler resumed his history with Cyrus' edict 538 B.C. (Ezr. 1:1-4). Cyrus the Persian, called the "King of Kings," had become the most powerful emperor in the world, with thirty provinces under him. He had met the Hebrew people when he captured the city of Babylon, to which they had been taken as slaves by Nebuchadnezzar. Cyrus was a wise and tolerant king; he did not believe in forcing his subjects into ways contrary to their customs, but respected their cultures and religious beliefs. And so it was fortunate that God's people, too, while in exile, were allowed to practice their religion in peace.

In his spirit of humaneness, Cyrus wrote this edict: "All the kingdoms of the earth the Lord, the God of heaven, has given to me, and he has also charged me to build him a house in Jerusalem, which is in Judah. Whoever, therefore, among you belongs to any part of his people, let him go up, and may his God be with him!" (Ezr. 1:2-3)

Everything happened just as the prophet Isaiah had foretold:

"I say of Cyrus: My shepherd,
 who fulfills my every wish;
He shall say of Jerusalem, 'Let her be rebuilt,'
 and of the temple, 'Let its foundations be laid' "
 (Is. 44:28).

The theme of the Chronicler is that Israel is a theocratic people, whose hope lies only in her fidelity to God—a God who does punish sin, but in order to correct sinners and not to destroy them. Moreover, He pardons the repentant and keeps His promises.

As soon as Cyrus had given permission, the first group of exiles returned to Palestine. For the most part these were not the same persons who had been deported, since after half a century of slavery a generation had died out; but they were their children and grandchildren, who loved their own country, and when God freed them they launched themselves into the unknown.

Back in Judea, they settled around Jerusalem. They found their country, once the center of David's and Solomon's glory, in disastrous condition and in part also occupied by pagans. It was a discouraging prospect, and soon families became so preoccupied with eking out a living that they lost interest in rebuilding the Temple. Finally, encouraged by the prophets Haggai, who prophesied that that Temple would see the glory of the Messiah (Hg. 2:1-9), and Zechariah, who prophesied the future greatness of Jerusalem (Zec. 8:1-8), and led by Zerubbabel, a descendant of David, they *did* rebuild the Lord's house. It took them almost five years, because of the hostility of the Samaritans, who looked upon Judah's territory as part of their own province and did not want the re-establishment of the Jewish state. But God was on the side of His chosen people. The Temple was completed in 515 B.C.

Later there arrived Ezra, the representative for Jewish affairs at the Persian court. More exiles returned with him. Ezra was a priest whose priesthood could be traced back to Aaron, the brother of Moses (Ezr. 7:1-5). He is also called "a scribe, well-versed in the law of Moses" (Ezr. 7:6), because he was especially dedicated to the study of the Law of God.

Ezra was given by King Artaxerxes I (464-423 B.C.) ample official authorization to foster the worship of the Lord in Judea and to re-establish the Mosaic Law in all its rigor as the constitution of the restored community, with power to impose severe penalties on those who did not obey it (Ezr. 7:25-26). Thus, he started by organizing the religious life of the community (Ezr. 7:1—8:36), by teaching the people the Law of the Lord, which they promised to keep (Neh. 8:1-8; 10:1), and by denouncing and promoting the dissolution of mixed marriages, condemned by the Law of Moses as "a snare and a trap for his people" (cf. Jos. 23:12-13; Ezr. 9:10).

Backing the reforms of Ezra was the layman, Nehemiah. Nehemiah was a well-educated Jew, cupbearer to King Artaxerxes. He too was permitted to return to his homeland (Neh. 1-6) with full royal authorization to rebuild the walls of Jerusalem, which had been destroyed by the Babylonians.

A man of willpower and faith in God, gifted with an excellent ability to organize, Nehemiah pleaded with the Judeans: "Come, let us rebuild the wall of Jerusalem, so that we may no longer be an object of derision!" (Neh. 2:17) The Jews responded in great number. The Samaritans kept ridiculing their efforts and plotted to come and fight against Jerusalem. "We prayed to our God," recorded Nehemiah in his *Memoirs,* "and posted a watch against them day and night" (Neh. 4:3). Then he continued, "I...addressed these words to the nobles, the magistrates, and the rest of the people: 'Have no fear of them! Keep in mind the Lord, who is great and to be feared, and fight for your brethren, your sons and daughters, your wives and your homes' " (Neh. 4:8). Within a few months Jerusalem was like a new city, fortified on all sides.

Appointed governor, Nehemiah concentrated on repopulating the city, introducing necessary administrative reforms, and stressing the Sabbath observance (Neh. 11-13).

These two great figures, Ezra and Nehemiah, were completely dedicated to the religious and political welfare of their people. They worked for one important purpose: to build Judaism's authentic way of life. Ezra was the religious reformer, the father of "post-exilic Judaism" with his three dominant concepts: the chosen race, the Temple, the Law. If his reforming ways were intransigent, this is to be seen within the context of his time, when the infant community needed strong spiritual unity and deep convictions, in order not to disintegrate when faced with Hellenism.

Nehemiah was the man of action and of trust in God, whose praises are sung by Ben Sirach:

"Extolled be the memory of Nehemiah!
  He rebuilt our ruined walls,
Restored our shattered defenses,
  and set up gates and bars" (Sir. 49:13).

Because of the unfailing courage of these two men, the morale of the people rose to new heights; they solemnly renewed the covenant with God, and promised to live a new life of adhesion to Him (Neh. 10:1-40).

The Chronicler wrote the Books of Ezra and Nehemiah around the same time that he wrote the Books of Chronicles. He used various and valuable sources, such as: the "Ezra Memoirs"; the "Nehemiah Memoirs"; other documents contemporary with the events recounted; lists of the returned exiles and of the population of Jerusalem; acts of the kings of Persia; and official letters and records from Persian sources. However, as in Chronicles, he is not mindful of the chronological order of the facts. He is selective and interpretive, and his work should be judged primarily as a work of theology. In fact, he has a religious purpose and fulfills it completely; that is, he presents the Jewish Restoration, and with it the reassurance that the remnant which has returned to Jerusalem is still the heir of God's promises.

There are beautiful lessons to be learned even from the long-past events recorded in the Books of Ezra and Nehemiah: fidelity to God, for instance, expressed by worshiping Him and keeping His commandments; patriotism, expressed by contributing to the welfare of one's nation; zeal in teaching the Word of God on the part of His ministers and religious; and generosity on the part of the laity in using their talents to cooperate with their leaders in the service of God and of His people.

STUDY QUESTIONS

1. *Who is the author of these two books?*
2. *Why are these books important from an historical point of view?*
3. *Who was Ezra and what did he accomplish?*
4. *Who was Nehemiah?*
5. *What are some of the lessons to be learned from these books?*

The Book of Tobit

The Book of Tobit is deuterocanonical. Until 1955, this book was available only in Greek manuscripts, the most faithful of which is the one appearing in the Codex Sinaiticus, from which the English translation was made. In 1955, a few Hebrew and Aramaic fragments of Tobit were discovered in Cave IV at Qumran, near the Dead Sea, a fact which confirms that its author wrote it either in Hebrew or Aramaic.

The name of the author is unknown, as is the place of the book's composition. The date of writing is difficult to establish, but scholars agree in placing it in the 2nd century B.C.

The inspired author used the literary form of a religious short story, with the purpose of conveying a variety of spiritual messages.

The many incongruities in matters of chronology, topography, and the time of actual events, only show that the author did not intend to write history but rather an interesting story. Thus, even though in the Catholic Bible Tobit is listed among the historical books, because of its content it is considered more a type of wisdom literature.

Using as a basis the biblical models of Genesis —Abraham and Sarah, Isaac and Rebekah, Jacob and Rachel—the inspired author writes his own new story. This story revolves around an ordinary Jewish family: its life and piety. The hero is Tobit, whom the author makes speak in the first person. Tobit is a formerly wealthy man of the tribe of Naphtali, living in exile in the city of Nineveh, with his wife Anna and his son Tobias. They had been deported during the exile of the northern tribes of Israel (721 B.C.) by the king of Assyria.

Tobit has been faithful to God from his youth, and even now in the pagan and hostile land of exile he is expressing his faith by serving the needs of his suffering compatriots with works of mercy. Tried by sorrow in the form of blindness in his old age, poor and ridiculed, he turns to God in prayer (Tb. 1:3-4). "Where are your charitable deeds now?" Tobit's wife tells him. "Where are your virtuous acts? See! Your true character is finally showing itself!" (Tb. 2:14) Deeply grieved in spirit, he prays that he might die (Tb. 3:1-6).

In the meantime, a young woman, Sarah, a relative of Tobit, in the distant land of Media, is also praying for death. She has lost seven husbands in succession, each killed on the wedding night by the demon Asmodeus (Tb. 3:7-8), and she too has become the object of criticism: "You are the one who strangles your husbands," a heartless maid is nagging Sarah. "Look at you! You have already been married seven times, but you have had no joy with any one of your husbands.... May we never see a son or daughter of yours!" (Tb. 3:7-9)

God answers the prayers of Tobit and Sarah, and in His own generous way! "At that very time," the story continues, "the prayer of these two suppliants was heard in the glorious presence of Almighty God. So Raphael [an angel in human form] was sent to heal them both" (Tb. 3:16).

It happens this way: that same day Tobit remembers the money he has lent to Gabael in Media. Thinking that now he will die, he calls his son, Tobias, gives him many wise instructions (Tb. 4:1-18) and concludes with this plea: "And now, son, I wish to inform you that I have deposited a great sum of money with Gabri's son Gabael at Rages in Media. Do not be discouraged, my child, because of our poverty. You will be a rich man if you fear God, avoid all sin, and do what is right before the Lord your God" (Tb. 4:20-21).

Tobias finds the Angel Raphael, sent by God to travel with him on his long trip through unfamiliar territory. Raphael brings him safely to Ecbatana, where the young man meets and marries Sarah.

This marriage is blessed by God with the expulsion of the demon Asmodeus, through the agency of the Angel Raphael. Also the marriage is described as an ideal Christian marriage:

"When the door was shut and the two were alone, Tobias got up from the bed and said, 'Sister, get up, and let us pray that the Lord may have mercy upon us.' And Tobias began to pray,

'Blessed are you, O God of our fathers,
and blessed be your holy and glorious name for ever.
Let the heavens and all your creatures bless you.
You made Adam and gave him Eve his wife
as a helper and support.
From them the race of mankind has sprung.
You said, "It is not good that the man should be alone;
let us make a helper for him like himself."
And now, O Lord, I am not taking this sister of mine because of lust, but with sincerity. Grant that I may find mercy and may grow old together with her.' And she said with him, 'Amen.' Then they both went to sleep for the night" (Tb. 8:4-9).*

Then Raphael collects the money, and they return to Nineveh with Sarah. Here Tobit is healed with medicine that Raphael has helped Tobias to obtain; the angel then discloses his identity and returns to heaven. Tobit thanks God with a song of praise:

"Now consider what [the Lord] has done for you,
and praise him with full voice....
In the land of my exile I praise him...
'Turn back, you sinners! do the right before him:
perhaps he may look with favor upon you
and show you mercy' " (Tb. 13:6).

Before dying, Tobit tells his son to leave Nineveh because God will destroy that sinful city. After the death of his parents, Tobias goes to Media with his family. Later he learns of the destruction of Nineveh.

In this pious story, which, according to some scholars, might have an historical basis, the author's themes stand out: the innocent who suffer, and the prayer which is heard. God wants to teach us to have faith during trials; to believe and to trust in His divine Providence, because He always takes care of all His children. It is true that sometimes He sends or permits trials, but in the end He always frees and rewards those who trust in Him.

Wise and very appropriate even today are Tobit's instructions to his son Tobias: "My son, when I die, bury me, and do not neglect your mother. Honor her all the days of your life, do what is pleasing to her, and do not grieve her. Remember, my son, that she faced many dangers for you while you were yet unborn. When she dies, bury her beside me in the same grave.

"Remember the Lord our God all your days, my son, and refuse to sin or to transgress his commandments. Live uprightly all the days of your life, and do not walk in the ways of wrongdoing. For if you do what is true, your ways will prosper through your deeds. Give alms from your possessions to all who live uprightly, and do not let your eye begrudge the gift when you make it. Do not turn your face away from any poor man, and the face of God will not be turned away from you. If you have many possessions, make your gift from them in proportion; if few, do not be afraid to give according to the little you have. So you will be laying up a good treasure for yourself against the day of necessity. For charity delivers from death and keeps you from entering the darkness; and for all who practice it charity is an excellent offering in the presence of the Most High.

"Beware, my son, of all immorality.

"Do not hold over till the next day the wages of any man who works for you, and pay him at once; and if you serve God you will receive payment.

"Watch yourself, my son, in everything you do, and be disciplined in all your conduct. And what you hate, do not do to any one. Do not drink wine to excess or let drunkenness go with you on your way. Give of your bread to the hungry, and of your clothing to the naked. Give all your surplus to charity, and do not let your eye begrudge the gift when you make it....

"Seek advice from every wise man, and do not despise any useful counsel. Bless the Lord God on every occasion; ask him that your ways may be made straight and that all your paths and plans may prosper. For none of the nations has understanding; but the Lord himself gives all good things, and according to his will he humbles whomever he wishes.

"So, my son, remember my commands, and do not let them be blotted out of your mind" (Tb. 4:3-12, 14-16, 18-19).*

Beautiful also are the farewell words of Raguel to his son-in-law, Tobias, and his daughter Sarah: " 'Good-bye, my son. Have a safe journey. May the Lord of heaven grant prosperity to you and to your wife Sarah. And may I see children of yours before I die!' Then he kissed his daughter Sarah and said to her: 'My daughter, honor your father-in-law and your mother-in-law, because from now on they are as much your parents as the ones who brought you into the world. Go in peace, my daughter; let me hear good reports about you as long as I live' " (Tb. 10:11-12).

Interwoven with prayers, psalms and words of wisdom, other themes are also discernible: the importance of keeping one's faith in a materialistic society; the virtues of family life; almsgiving; duties towards the dead; the role of Christian marriage; and more.

The Book of Tobit is also among the most important of the books of the Old Testament for angelology—the doctrine of the angels as faithful ministers of Divine Providence.

Once again, before closing, a practical lesson of this story comes from the angel's mouth, addressed to Tobit and in him to all of us: "Praise God, do good, pray, fast, give alms" (cf. Tb. 12:6-10).

STUDY QUESTIONS
1. *What is the literary form of the Book of Tobit?*
2. *Approximately when was this book written?*
3. *What are some of the virtues that Tobit himself shows?*
4. *Point out other lessons taught in this book.*

The Book of Judith

The Book of Judith, like the Book of Tobit, is deuterocanonical, that is to say, it was recognized by the Church only after some disputes in the early years of the Christian era. However, the Council of Trent reaffirmed this book's place in the Catholic canon. The Jews did not include Judith in their canon, but they did adopt it to be read at the feast of Hanukkah.

Presently, the Book of Judith is extant in Greek. Scholars agree, however, that the Greek edition is a translation from a Semitic language, probably Hebrew.

The author was a Jew who wrote the book about the year 150 B.C., perhaps in Palestine. This can be deduced from his knowledge of Greek customs (3:7, 15:13) and his emphasis on legal prescriptions proper to that time.

The inspired author wrote for the purpose of encouraging his compatriots, who were then undergoing the persecution begun by the Seleucid king, Antiochus Epiphanes. The Seleucid dynasty had gained dominion over Palestine in 198 B.C. Several of these rulers were determined to wipe out Judaism, replacing it with pagan Hellenistic culture.

A reader who knows ancient history can see why most scholars today agree that Judith may not be considered an historical book. The author, in fact, shows absolute indifference when he writes about persons, dates, places.... He mingles actual events with others of different epochs. He calls Nebuchadnezzar king of Assyria, reigning in the city of Nineveh, while instead he was king of Babylon and resided there. The town of Bethulia, around which the drama revolves, cannot be located or even identified.

"Why, then," one might ask, "are there seven chapters of history and geography in the beginning of the book?" One opinion is that the author did this deliberately, in order more forcefully to focus the attention of the reader on the religious drama and its solution. Thus, as the Book of Tobit, so also the Book of Judith is considered a didactic story. (Whether or not it is built upon actual events, we have no way of knowing.)

The theme of the book is God's Providence. The author wanted to convey a message: The Jews of the post-exilic period needed to remember again that their God was the very same all-powerful God of the Exodus, who successfully defied the Pharaoh and led their forefathers out of Egypt by the hand of Moses. Now the same almighty God is still with His people to help them, as long as they keep His covenant and turn to Him with full confidence and humble prayer.

In the form of this vivid story, God illustrates how He is the God of history. In fact, in a desperate situation, the Most High delivers His people by the hand of a woman, Judith, who becomes God's agent for the protection of the Temple of Jerusalem, and of the People of God.

The tiny Jewish nation faces the mighty army of General Holofernes, whose plan is to conquer all nations and destroy all religions, to have the whole world worship the deified Nebuchadnezzar (chapters 1-3). The Jews resist and are, therefore, besieged in Bethulia. But when the water supply fails, they are at the point of surrender (chapters 4-7). When the situation is absolutely hopeless, Judith appears (8:1-12, 20). Her name means "Jewess," representative of the Jewish nation.

Judith is a very beautiful, devout and courageous young widow, whose life is spent in prayer and charity. Judith rebukes the leaders for their lack of faith in God, and she reminds her discouraged countrymen that this lack of faith may bring disgraceful defeat just when God is ready to grant a glorious victory, provided they pray and keep His Law. Judith reasserts Achior's thesis: So long as Israel remains loyal to God, she is invincible.

God will defend Israel because He has set her apart and she is consecrated. Israel's strength, in fact, lies in what this world calls "weakness," that is: faith and prayer.

Judith fasts, prays, adorns herself and presents herself to Holofernes. The general is enchanted by her charm. But while he is full of wine and sleeps soundly, she cuts off his head. The Assyrians, panic-stricken, run away. The war ends with the victory and triumph of the Jews (13:1-15, 25). They sing the praises of Judith and go to Jerusalem for a solemn thanksgiving.

"You are the glory of Jerusalem,
 the surpassing joy of Israel;
 You are the splendid boast of our people" (15:9).

Today these words are used in the liturgy of the Church in regard to the Blessed Virgin Mary, who defeats the enemy of our salvation, the devil.

The entire content of this small book of Judith is centered in this belief: Fidelity to God is a sure pledge of His help (5:5-21). The Almighty, who created the world with a word, always listens to the prayers of the humble and accomplishes marvels for them (16:13-15).

STUDY QUESTIONS

1. *Approximately when was the book of Judith written?*
2. *What was the purpose of this book?*
3. *How can we explain the sacred writer's indifference to history and geography?*
4. *How can the content of this book be summarized?*

The Book of Esther

As the Book of Judith does, the Book of Esther narrates the liberation of the chosen people through the mediation of a woman: Esther, a Jewish heroine.

Through the clever action of his first and powerful minister, Haman the Agagite, the king of Persia, Ahasuerus (Xerxes), 485-464 B.C., had signed an edict condemning to death in a single day all the Jews throughout his vast empire, an empire comprising one hundred twenty-seven provinces. The reason for this was Haman's desire to take revenge on the Jewish servant, Mordecai, who, for personal, national, or religious motives, had refused to bow to him. Thus, Haman had spoken evil to the King about all of Israel. But Mordecai turned to his niece and adopted daughter, Esther, who, fortunately, had been chosen as a wife by the king himself, in place of Vashti.

At first Queen Esther was afraid, but relying on the two effective means of penance and prayer, she acted resolutely. She revealed to Ahasuerus the malicious plans of Haman. Thus the royal decree of extermination of the Jews was promptly revoked; Haman and the other enemies of the Jews were condemned to death, and Mordecai himself was chosen to replace Haman as first minister of the land. The wonderful event was celebrated with a great feast and much joy.

The story of Esther was perpetuated with the annual observance of the feast of the Purim (lots), called thus because the day of the extermination of the Jews had been decided by lot. This feast, whose real origin is not known, would remind the Jewish people of succeeding ages that God can overcome evil and deliver His people who trust in Him.

The Book of Esther is divided as follows:
1. A brief prologue (11:2-12 and 12:1-6)
2. Esther becomes a queen (1:1-2, 18)
3. Mordecai and Haman (2:19—3:13; 13:1-7; 3:14—4:8)
4. The intervention of Esther (13:1-3; 4:9-17; 13:8-14, 19; 13:4-19; 5:1-8, 12)
5. The promulgation and the execution of the decree in favor of the Jews (16:1-24; 8:13-17; 9:1-32; 10:1-13; 11:1)

The book illustrates how the ancient world hated the Jewish people because of their different way of life, consisting in fidelity to the Law of God. Because of this fidelity, or because of their repentance, God always protected them and intervened at the right time to take care of them.

This little book has come down to us in two substantially different forms: one in Hebrew, the other one (in the Septuagint) in Greek.

The Hebrew text is considered by most scholars to be original. It is found in the Hebrew Bible, and it is very popular among the Jews themselves, even in our days. They read it during the feast of Purim. It is one of five *megillot* (scrolls), which are read entirely, each on one of the principle Jewish feastdays.

The Greek text is a free translation of the Hebrew text. It has an addition of 107 verses dealing with: the dream of Mordecai; the two edicts of Ahasuerus; the prayer of Mordecai and of Esther; a second account of Esther's appeal to Ahasuerus and an appendix.

How and when these verses were added, and where they came from, scholars are still studying. St. Jerome seemed to think that they were the author's reflections while he was choosing the material for his story among the historical sources. In his Vulgate he put them together as an appendix. The New American Bible inserts them into the shorter text and labels each chapter of them: A, B, C, etc. The Jerusalem Bible, too, leaves them where they are in the Greek text, but in italic type without any division into chapters and verses. These additions repeatedly attribute Israel's liberation to Divine Providence and give ethnic and religious causes for the persecution. Even though they are deuterocanonical, the Church has accepted them as equally inspired with the rest of the book and therefore the Word of God.

The author of the Book of Esther is an unknown Jew, living either in Susa (Persia) or in Palestine. He wrote between the late fifth century and the late second century B.C. According to 2 Maccabees 15:36, the Hebrew text was in existence by 160 B.C. At that time the Palestinians were celebrating Mordecai's Day; this fact presupposes that the story of Esther was already known. The Greek version was already known in 114 B.C., when it was sent to the Jews in Egypt to authenticate the feast of Purim—its origin, meaning and date, the fourteenth and fifteenth of Adar (February-March).

It cannot be said up to what point the Book of Esther is historical and at what point it is not, but there is no justification for interpreting the story in mythological or cultic terms.

As did the authors of Tobit and Judith, the author of Esther uses chronology and historical elements very freely. He has written a didactic book with a religious thesis, namely: God's Providence continually watches over His people and never abandons them if they are faithful to Him or return to Him in sincere repentance. The main part of the message is contained in 10:9, "God remembered his people and rendered justice to his inheritance." There is no need to be surprised at the vindictive tone of this little book. We are to remember that Jesus' command to love our enemies had not yet been taught by His word and example.

STUDY QUESTIONS

1. *What, in general, is the story of the Book of Esther?*
2. *What is unusual about the composition of this book as it is found in Catholic Bibles?*
3. *What is the message of the Book of Esther?*

The First and Second Books of Maccabees

There are four books known by the title "Maccabees," the last two of which, however, are apocryphal.

The title *Maccabees* properly belongs to the hero, Judas Maccabeus. Its meaning is debated: Perhaps it derives from the Hebrew form *maqqabyāhū*, meaning "designated by God," or, as some interpreters understand, "the hammer" striking the enemy. This surname had become the proper name of Judas (1 Mc. 5:34) and later on was extended to the whole family of Mattathias and to their descendants.

After the death of Alexander the Great (323 B.C.), his vast empire had been divided among numerous claimants. In the Middle East the two most important kingdoms were Syria, with Antioch as its capital, governed by the dynasty of the Seleucids, and Egypt, with Alexandria as its capital, governed by the Ptolemies. Between these two kingdoms lay Palestine, which belonged to Egypt until 200 B.C. and then passed under the dominion of the Seleucids. Antiochus III and Seleucus IV exercised religious tolerance with regard to Palestine; Antiochus IV Epiphanes, instead, initiated a struggle to impose religious and social uniformity on the entire kingdom. Thus the Hebrews were subjected to a series of pagan cults repugnant to the religious conscience of the more devout. However, even in the midst of the chosen people many were in favor of the Hellenistic religion; they sacrificed to idols and profaned the Sabbath. They actively collaborated for the realization of the desires of Antiochus.

The two Books of Maccabees narrate the national and religious insurrection promoted by a family, the family of the priest Mattathias, who initiated the Jewish revolt against the Seleucids in 167 B.C. When the officers of Antiochus IV in charge of enforcing the apostasy came to the city of Modein to organize the pagan sacrifices, Mattathias and his sons refused: "Heaven preserve us from forsaking the Law and its observances. As for the king's orders, we will not follow them: we will not swerve from our own religion either to right or to left" (1 Mc. 2:21-22).**

The first book embraces a period of 40 years, from the accession of Antiochus IV until the death of Simon, the last brother of Judas. It is divided as follows:

Historical introduction (1:1—2:70);
Judas (3:1—9:22);
Jonathan (9:23—12:53);
Simon (13:1—16:24).

Little is known about the author. From the book itself we know that he is a Jew, a fervent nationalist, and probably an eyewitness, at least in part, of Judas' heroic deeds. We know that he wrote his book near the end of the 2nd century B.C. and certainly before the year 63 B.C. (when Pompey captured Jerusalem), because he praises the Romans (1 Mc. 8). Scholars also generally agree that he wrote in Hebrew and that the book was translated into Greek, in which language it has come down to us.

As for its literary form, 1 Maccabees is an historical book, composed with the criteria proper to semitic historiography, already encountered in the Books of Judges, Samuel and Kings. It quotes numerous official documents. The author, however, emphasizes the religious significance of the events which he sets forth. He meant to convey a lesson for every Israelite to learn: Fidelity to the Law and faith in God can accomplish more than a great number of soldiers (2:61-64).

As for doctrinal content, the Law is at the center of all events: The battle is not so much between Seleucids and Israelites, between the Gentile kingdoms and the Hebrew kingdom, but rather between observers and profaners of the Law. 1 Maccabees shows that it is supreme glory to die fighting for the Law (2:64). This is what practically all the heroes of this book did.

The second book is the work of an epitomist, who declares that he is summing up the five books of Jason of Cyrene. This work is not a continuation of the first book, but runs parallel to it in part: It starts with the end of the reign of Seleucus IV, father of Antiochus Epiphanes, and ends with the defeat of Nicanor. It spans only 15 years, the same length of time covered in the first seven chapters of 1 Maccabees. 2 Maccabees predates the other book. It was written in Greek in the land of Egypt.

In the introduction (1:1—2:18), the author quotes in full two letters of the inhabitants of Jerusalem, with which they invite their brethren in Egypt to celebrate the feast of the Dedication.

After having quoted the letters, the author describes the work which he is about to begin: It has cost him much effort; he has had to read and summarize the difficult books of Jason; and, seeking to set forth a work pleasing to his readers, he has permitted himself to take a few liberties in regard to his source.

This second book is developed in five parts, whose center of perspective is always the Temple:

1) The holiness of the Temple is inviolable—the episode of Heliodorus during the supreme pontificate of Onias (chapter 3);

2) God abandons His Temple to profanation to punish the sins of infidelity committed by the priests Jason and Menelaus (chapters 4-7).

3) The faithful Judas purifies the Temple (8—10:8).

4) Lysias, representative of Eupator, offers sacrifices in the Temple (10:10—13:26);

5) Judas overcomes and kills Nicanor, blasphemer and profaner of the Temple. An annual feast is instituted to commemorate the victory of Judas (14:1—15:37).

At this point the author modestly takes leave of his reader (15:38-39).

The literary form is oratorical: The author wants to instruct and persuade. Thus, more than history in the ordinary meaning of the term, he writes an edifying story, to show the victory of Palestinian Jews against their pagan enemy, and to strengthen the faith of the Jews by appealing to the heroic examples of their brethren (6:31). He knows history, but because of his religious purpose, he redistributes the events, inserts stories, magnifies numbers.

The doctrinal content of 2 Maccabees is more developed than the theology of 1 Maccabees. The author describes God as king—kind, provident, just, omnipotent and eternal (1:25)—the Creator of all (7:28). He dwells among His people in His Temple (14:35-36) and watches over them.

The author stresses the primacy of God's Law. If the Jews observe it, particularly the Sabbath (8:27; 15:1-4), God will be merciful to them (8:27). But toward the ungodly He is a just judge (12:6). When calamities occur, Israel has only itself to blame (4:10-17; 6:12-16; 7:18; 10:4; 12:40-41). Penance, however, can restore the bond of friendship between God and His people (7:32-33, 37-38; 8:5; 12:42-45).

God helps His just ones. He is their defender (7:6; 8:36; 12:11). His help can be sought in prayer and sacrifice (3:22). Whoever dies in a holy battle (12:45) or in persecution is a martyr (chapters 6-7). The impious will be punished (5:9-10; 7:13-14, 17, 19, 35; 9:18; 13:7-8). Intercessory prayer is presented as a means with which one can help the departed brethren (12:44-45).

This book also presents the clearest Old Testament teaching on the resurrection of the dead (7:9); they will rise with bodies fully restored (7:11); but for the wicked, there will be no resurrection to life (7:14); rather, God will punish them (7:17).

Both Books of Maccabees are called deuterocanonical. They are not accepted in the Hebrew canon. Even though Protestants follow the Jewish canon, they have great esteem for these books.

Such Church Fathers and other ecclesiastical writers as Clement of Alexandria, Hippolytus, Tertullian, Origen, St. Cyprian, Eusebius of Caesarea, St. Jerome, St. Augustine and Theodoret cite these two books as Holy Scripture.

The Church declared them inspired by God in the Provincial Councils of Hippo (393) and Carthage (397, 419) and in the General Councils of Florence (1441), Trent (1546) and Vatican I (1870).

STUDY QUESTIONS

1. *To whom does the title "Maccabees" properly belong? To whom has it been extended?*
2. *What is "Maccabeus" thought to mean?*
3. *What position did devout Hebrews find themselves in under Antiochus IV?*
4. *What do we know about the author of 1 Maccabees?*
5. *What is the literary form of Maccabees and what is its theme?*
6. *Describe the literary form and doctrinal content of 2 Maccabees.*
7. *Compare 2 Maccabees with 1 Maccabees.*

The Book of Job

The theme of the Book of Job is the problem of the suffering of the innocent, and of retribution.

Job is a faithful servant of God. He is wise, rich and happy. God permits Satan to test him to see if he will remain faithful and strong in his faith in spite of all his sufferings and the disasters which befall him.

Three of his friends come to sympathize with Job. But all three defend the traditional belief that if Job suffers, it is because he has sinned. Appealing to his conscience, Job protests his innocence repeatedly; he even questions God, but he does not say any impious word.

A fourth and younger friend appears, too. He reproves Job and his friends and justifies God's ways (chapters 32-37): "Surely, God cannot act wickedly, the Almighty cannot violate justice" (34:12).

At this point God intervenes directly (chapters 38-41). He does not justify His actions, but he does reveal Himself to Job as the almighty Creator of all things—inanimate and animate—as their Lawgiver, the infinitely intelligent, personal Being, the only One behind all that is happening in the universe.

Job has challenged God. Now God challenges Job, confronting him with the mystery of His wisdom and goodness, manifest in all His works (chapters 40-41). Job is overwhelmed with this new manifestation of God's true nature and realizes his foolishness for having spoken to Him so irreverently. First, he remains silent, then he bows down before the Almighty and prays:

"I know that you can do all things,
 and that no purpose of yours can be thwarted.
'Who is this that hides counsel without knowledge?'

Therefore I have uttered what I did not understand,
   things too wonderful for me, which I did not know.
'Hear, and I will speak;
   I will question you, and you declare to me.'
I had heard of you by the hearing of the ear,
   but now my eye sees you;
therefore I despise myself,
   and repent in dust and ashes" (Job 42:2-6).*

After Job has taken this attitude of penance, humility and trust, God restores his former possessions twofold.

The Book of Job has a didactic purpose. Today, too, the just suffer. But they know that even when the depths of God's wisdom and goodness cannot be explored, yet they are to trust in Him, because God has a good reason for everything, a fatherly reason. However, He is also the almighty and just God, and therefore the just are to wait without complaining, because reward will certainly follow!

St. Augustine says, "Since God is supremely good, He would not permit any evil at all in His works, unless He were sufficiently almighty and good to bring good even from evil." It is therefore a mark of the limitless goodness of God that He permits evils to exist, and draws good from them.

STUDY QUESTIONS

1. What is the main topic of this book?
2. What is the book's lesson?

The Book of Psalms

The Book of Psalms, or *Psalter,* is the prayerbook of the Bible. The Psalter is a collection of one hundred fifty songs or hymns used by the chosen people of God in the Temple of Jerusalem and in their synagogues. Tradition attributes many of them to David.

Before the collectors arranged these psalms in their present order, numerous smaller collections existed. This explains why some psalms are duplicated almost word for word. The present collection is divided into five books. A short doxology, or verse of praise, marks the end of each book (41:13; 72:18-20; 89:51; 106:48; 150:1-6).

Most important of all is the fact that the psalms were the *prayers* of the Old Testament, inspired by God Himself. Thus, they are the best prayers, containing abundant spiritual riches. They are most varied in form and content: Many are prayers of supplication or petition to God for His help in spiritual and temporal needs; numerous also are hymns of thanksgiving and praise to God for what He is and what He has done. Other psalms speak about the future Messiah and almost describe Him. Still others are wisdom psalms, in which one listens to God instead of speaking to Him. There are also the so-called "imprecatory" or "cursing" psalms. The basic fact needed for understanding these latter is the background in which they originated. The Old Testament was preparatory to the New Testament, and the love of one's enemies had not yet been prescribed. We are to pray these psalms in the spirit of Jesus.

In New Testament times the psalms were recited by Jesus Himself, by the Virgin Mary, by the Apostles and by the early Christians. In the catacombs and throughout Christian history, the psalms have been the prayerbook of the Church, the new People of God. Today countless Christians the world over pray the psalms, which from the beginning the Church has incorporated unchanged into her official prayer, or liturgy.

Even though the psalms reflect the psalmists' personal experiences and the events of their own times, they have a universal note because they were inspired by God, who knows our hearts' deepest emotions in all the vicissitudes of varying times and ages. They thus express the attitude towards God that each of us should have.

INTRODUCTIONS TO EACH OF THE 150 PSALMS

Psalm 1 *True Happiness*
This psalm introduces the entire Psalter and anticipates its theme: the lot of the good and that of the wicked.

Psalm 2 *The Universal Reign of the Messiah*
This psalm vividly depicts history as a battle between the army of God and His people and the army of evil, which opposes the plans of God.

Psalm 3 *Trust in God in Time of Danger*
In the face of all the threats of his persecutors and despite his miserable outward situation, David declares himself sure of God's protection.

Psalm 4 *Joyful Confidence in God*
This psalm radiates a sense of security and joy.

Psalm 5 *Prayer for Divine Help*
In response to his morning prayer, the psalmist experiences the divine protection.

Psalm 6 *Prayer in Time of Distress*
The psalmist finds himself oppressed by a serious sickness, which he regards as a divine punishment because of his faults. This is the first of the seven penitential psalms.

Psalm 7 *An Appeal to the Divine Judge*
This is the prayer of an innocent man who has been calumniated.

Psalm 8 *The Majesty of God and the Dignity of Man*
First the psalmist contrasts man's littleness with God's greatness. Then he praises the Lord for the dignity and power which He has given to man.

Psalm 9 *Thanksgiving for the Overthrow of Hostile Nations*
This psalm is chiefly a prayer against the enemies of Israel.

Psalm 10 *Prayer for Help Against Oppressors*
The psalmist asks for deliverance from the wicked among God's people.

Psalm 11 *Unshaken Confidence in God*
This psalm expresses hope in the all-knowing God, who rewards justly.

Psalm 12 *Prayer Against Evil Tongues*
The psalmist asks God's help against the deceitful and proud.

Psalm 13 *Prayer of One in Sorrow*
This is the plea of one who is oppressed by his enemies yet still trusts in God's help.

Psalm 14 *A Lament over Widespread Corruption*
Evil is spreading. As the psalmist prays for his people, he foretells the punishment of the godless.

Psalm 15 *The Guest of God*
This psalm summarizes twelve conditions necessary for living in peace with the Lord.

Psalm 16 *God the Supreme Good*
The psalmist pledges his loyalty to God, of whose presence he is constantly aware.

Psalm 17 *Prayer Against Persecutors*
This is an appeal for God's just judgment in behalf of the innocent.

Psalm 18 *Thanksgiving for Help and Victory*
The psalmist praises God for having enabled him to triumph over his enemies.

Psalm 19 *God's Glory in the Heavens and in the Law*
This psalm consists of two distinct parts—the first praising the perfection of God's universe and the second that of His moral law.

Psalm 20 *Prayer for the King in Time of War*
The psalmist asks God's blessings for the king as he goes into battle.

Psalm 21 *Thanksgiving and Prayers for the King*
This is the complement of Psalm 20. God is praised for the victory He has granted to the king.

Psalm 22 *Passion and Triumph of the Messiah*
This is one of the most revered of all the psalms. Unquestionably messianic, it was quoted by Jesus as He hung on the cross and reveals the essence of the Savior's mission as the Suffering Servant described in the book of Isaiah.

Psalm 23 *The Lord, Shepherd and Host*
Another favorite, this psalm uses the images of a shepherd and a generous host to describe God's loving care.

Psalm 24 *The Lord's Solemn Entry into Zion*
This psalm recalls the procession which brought the ark of the covenant into Jerusalem and the sanctuary.

Psalm 25 *Prayer for Guidance and Help*
This psalm has three main parts. The first and third are petitions; the second, a meditation on God's goodness.

Psalm 26 *Prayer of an Innocent Man*
The psalmist protests his innocence and begs God not to number him among the wicked.

Psalm 27 *Trust in God*
This psalm consists of two distinct parts. In the first, the psalmist asserts his confidence that God will deliver

him from his enemies and expresses longing for the shelter of the Temple. In the second, he calls on the Lord to guide and protect him.

Psalm 28 *Petition and Thanksgiving*
The psalmist asks not to be punished with the wicked, then thanks the Lord in advance for having heard him.

Psalm 29 *God's Majesty in the Storm*
Some think that this psalm was an ancient Canaanite hymn, adapted by the Hebrews for worship of the Lord in His Temple.

Psalm 30 *Thanksgiving for Deliverance from Death*
The psalmist expresses his gratitude for recovery from a grave illness.

Psalm 31 *Prayer in Distress and Thanksgiving for Escape*
The first two sections of this psalm describe the misery of the psalmist and his hope for God's help. The third section expresses thanks to the Lord for favors that have been, or are to be, received.

Psalm 32 *Remission of Sin*
The sinner's remorse gives him no peace until he confesses his sins and experiences the joy of God's pardon. This is the second of the seven penitential psalms.

Psalm 33 *Praise of the Lord's Power and Providence*
The psalmist invites the just to chant God's praises because of His faithfulness, power, wisdom, knowledge and goodness.

Psalm 34 *Praise of God, the Protector of the Just*
This is a psalm of gratitude.

Psalm 35 *Prayer for Help Against Unjust Enemies*
The psalmist calls upon God for help and, after describing the wrongs done by his enemies, he repeats his plea.

Psalm 36 *Human Wickedness and Divine Providence*
The psalmist prays to be delivered from wicked men, who forget or ignore the punishments that the provident but just God will send because of their sins.

Psalm 37 *The Fate of Sinners and the Reward of the Just*
This psalm deals with the tremendous "problem of evil"—why the wicked may enjoy prosperity in this life while the good frequently suffer. Old Testament revelation on this point was incomplete; in the light of the New Testament this problem becomes less difficult.

Psalm 38 *Prayer of an Afflicted Sinner*
The psalmist is almost overwhelmed by the burden of his sins. This is the third of the penitential psalms.

Psalm 39 *The Brevity and Vanity of Life*
The psalmist laments the transitory human condition aggravated by sin, yet he hopes for pardon and help from God.

Psalm 40 *Gratitude and Prayer for Help*
Consisting of two distinct parts, this psalm may be considered as an expression of thanksgiving for past blessings and a petition for help in present miseries.

Psalm 41 *Thanksgiving after Sickness*
This psalm exalts compassion for the needy and recalls God's goodness to the psalmist during an illness.

Psalm 42 *Desire for God and His Temple*
From exile, the psalmist directs his thoughts to God's sanctuary at Jerusalem. This psalm is one of the most lyric poems in the Bible.

Psalm 43 *Longing for God's Temple*
This psalm continues the thought of Psalm 42, to which it must have been joined at one time.

Psalm 44 *Israel's Past Glory and Present Need*

This psalm contrasts present humiliation with former grandeur and ends with an appeal for God's mercy.

Psalm 45 *Nuptial Ode for the Messianic King*

Apparently this psalm was composed for the marriage of a Davidic ruler with a foreign princess. Because of its clear allusions to the messianic promise made by God to the House of David, both Hebrews and Christians have retained this joyful song as part of the Psalter.

Psalm 46 *God the Refuge of Israel*

This psalm is a patriotic victory hymn; Jerusalem has been delivered from a grave danger.

Psalm 47 *The Lord, the King of All Nations*

This is another hymn of triumph for a victory obtained by Israel through the powerful help of God.

Psalm 48 *Thanksgiving for Jerusalem's Deliverance*

After one of the many enemy attacks repulsed by the people of Jerusalem, this hymn of thanksgiving was sung in the Temple.

Psalm 49 *The Vanity of Worldly Riches*

Again the psalmist wrestles with the problem of evil: Why do the wicked prosper? He concludes that this prosperity will not last; death will be accompanied by ruin.

Psalm 50 *The Acceptable Sacrifice*

God Himself tells His people in what true worship consists.

Psalm 51 *The Miserere: Prayer of Repentance*

Replete with an exquisite religious sense, this psalm has become a classic Christian hymn of repentance. It is the fourth of the penitential psalms.

Psalm 52 *The Deceitful Tongue*

This psalm seems to refer to the treachery of one of David's enemies, who shed much innocent blood.

Psalm 53 *Lament over Widespread Corruption*
Concerned with failure to observe the moral law, this psalm is almost identical with Psalm 14.

Psalm 54 *Confident Prayer in Great Peril*
The psalmist asks the Lord to deliver him from danger and promises a sacrifice of thanksgiving.

Psalm 55 *Complaint Against Enemies and a Disloyal Companion*
The psalmist laments the doings of his enemies and the treachery of a former friend. He confidently implores God's help.

Psalm 56 *Trust in God, the Helper in Need*
This is another confident plea for the deliverance of the psalmist from his enemies.

Psalm 57 *Confident Prayer for Deliverance*
This psalm consists of two parts, each of which begins with a trusting plea for help and ends with a refrain to God's glory.

Psalm 58 *Against Unjust Judges*
The psalmist calls upon God to punish the judges who do not administer true justice.

Psalm 59 *Against Bloodthirsty Enemies*
This psalm consists of two similar parts, in which the psalmist asks God to deliver him from his wicked enemies, whom he compares to ravenous dogs.

Psalm 60 *Prayer After Defeat in Battle*
The psalmist thanks God for saving a remnant of the defeated army and places his trust in the Lord's future assistance.

Psalm 61 *Prayer of the King in Exile*
The exile longs for God's help and protection, confident that his prayers will be heard.

Psalm 62 *Trust in God Alone*
The psalmist is confident in God's protection, despite the attacks of his enemies.

Psalm 63 *Ardent Longing for God*
Far from Mount Zion, where he was accustomed to pour out his heart before the invisible presence of Yahweh enthroned on the ark, the devout psalmist longs to be able to return to Jerusalem and again worship in the sanctuary.

Psalm 64 *Treacherous Conspirators Punished by God*
The psalmist prays for God's help against his calumniators.

Psalm 65 *Thanksgiving for God's Blessings*
The people thank God for abundant rains and rich harvests.

Psalm 66 *Praise of God, Israel's Deliverer*
This psalm consists of two distinct parts—one of gratitude for God's providence during the Exodus and in a recent national calamity; the other, of thanksgiving for individual benefits.

Psalm 67 *Harvest Prayer That All Men May Worship God*
This psalm calls upon all men to praise the Lord.

Psalm 68 *God's Triumphal Procession*
This psalm, which opens with the ancient war cry of Israel, was written to be sung when the ark of the covenant was carried into the Temple in solemn procession. It is a lyric resumé of the glorious past of Israel.

Psalm 69 *A Cry of Anguish in Great Distress*
Like Psalm 22, this psalm is a plea for God's help in a situation of unmerited misery and disgrace. Many verses of it are quoted in the New Testament with reference to Christ.

Psalm 70 *Prayer for Divine Help*
This brief psalm expresses the psalmist's firm trust in God, whose help he implores.

Psalm 71 *Humble Prayer in Time of Old Age*
Each of the three sections of this psalm expresses humble confidence in God.

Psalm 72 *The Kingdom of the Messiah*
This psalm is of great importance because of its description of the Messiah and His reign. Many expressions find their complete fulfillment only in Christ.

Psalm 73 *The False Happiness of the Wicked*
As did Psalms 37 and 49, this psalm inquires into the prosperity of the wicked. The conclusion is that God will destroy the wicked but will receive the just into glory.

Psalm 74 *Prayer in Time of National Calamity*
This psalm probably refers to the burning of Jerusalem and its Temple by the Babylonians under Nebuchadnezzar.

Psalm 75 *God, the Just Judge of the Wicked*
The psalmist praises God for the true justice that He will exercise over the wicked.

Psalm 76 *Thanksgiving for the Overthrow of Israel's Foes*
This is a hymn of triumph, in which Israel's victory is attributed chiefly to God.

Psalm 77 *Lament and Comfort in Time of Distress*
The psalmist raises his sorrowful voice to God in a time of profound desolation for Israel—perhaps during the Babylonian Exile. From memories of the past, he derives a ray of hope for the future.

Psalm 78 *God's Goodness Despite Israel's Ingratitude*
This is a meditation on the history of Israel, a great hymn to the story of salvation, with useful lessons for the present and the future.

Psalm 79 *The Destruction of Jerusalem and Its Temple*
This psalm probably recalls the seizure and destruction of Jerusalem by the Babylonians.

Psalm 80 *Prayer for the Restoration of the Lord's Vineyard*

Using the symbol of God's vine, referring to Israel, the psalmist laments the devastation wrought by a foreign invasion, recalls God's past kindness, and implores deliverance while pledging renewed fidelity.

Psalm 81 *Festive Song with an Admonition to Fidelity*

This psalm consists of two distinct sections—the first, a short song sung on the Feast of Booths; the second, an admonition from God to be faithful to Him.

Psalm 82 *Judgment Against Wicked Judges*

The psalmist presents God as passing sentence on unjust judges.

Psalm 83 *Prayer Against a Hostile Alliance*

This is an invocation against enemies. Ten traditional enemies of God's people are named.

Psalm 84 *Desire for the Sanctuary*

This may have been one of the "pilgrim songs" sung by groups journeying to Jerusalem for the great feasts.

Psalm 85 *Prayer for Complete Restoration*

This psalm may have been composed in the period of restoration after the Exile. The people have received blessings from God, yet still suffer hardships and look for better days.

Psalm 86 *Prayer in Time of Distress*

This psalm consists of supplications for help combined with a short hymn of praise.

Psalm 87 *Zion, the Home of All Nations*

This is a prophetic vision of messianic Jerusalem, which will be the spiritual home of all nations and the source of all good for everyone.

Psalm 88 *Lament and Prayer in Affliction*

The psalmist, who is mortally ill, bewails his misery and seeming abandonment by God.

Psalm 89   *Prayer for the Fulfillment of God's Promises to David*

This psalm is a pious lament regarding the divine promises made to the house of David and the almost total ruin that has come upon it.

Psalm 90   *God's Eternity and Man's Frailty*

In this meditation on the brevity and misery of life, the psalmist sees suffering and death as punishments for sin.

Psalm 91   *Security Under God's Protection*

This is a song of trust in God's protection amid all the mishaps of life.

Psalm 92   *Praise of God's Just Government of Mankind*

This hymn extols the divine justice and promises happiness to the upright.

Psalm 93   *The Glory of the Lord's Kingdom*

The psalmist exalts the everlasting stability of the kingdom of the divine Ruler.

Psalm 94   *A Warning to Israel's Oppressors*

This is a fervent, confident prayer for the punishment of the wicked and the triumph of righteousness.

Psalm 95   *A Call to Praise and Obedience*

This psalm invites all to worship the Lord, our King and Shepherd. It concludes with a warning to be faithful.

Psalm 96   *The Glories of the Lord, the King of the Universe*

This psalm opens with the words, "Sing to the Lord a new song." The song is truly new, because of its universal ideal: The world and all its peoples are invited to adore the one, true God.

Psalm 97   *The Divine King, the Just Judge of All*

The opening stanza of this psalm portrays the coming of God as judge. Israel rejoices to see the overthrow of paganism and the reward of true worshipers of God.

Psalm 98 *The Lord, the Victorious King and Just Judge*

The opening verses of this psalm refer to a great intervention by God in behalf of His people. All nations and all creation are invited to welcome the Savior with joy.

Psalm 99 *The Lord, the Holy King*

This hymn of praise especially emphasizes the *holiness* of God.

Psalm 100 *Processional Hymn*

This hymn was sung at the solemn entry into the Temple, probably in connection with the offering of a thanksgiving sacrifice.

Psalm 101 *Norm of Life for Rulers*

This is the prayerful resolution of a davidic king, perhaps written at the beginning of his reign or for some special occasion.

Psalm 102 *Prayer in Time of Distress*

This psalm seems to consist of two distinct parts: a personal lament and a prayer for the restoration of Zion. It is the fifth of the seven penitential psalms.

Psalm 103 *Praise of Divine Goodness*

Basically a hymn of thanksgiving, this psalm reflects concepts close to those of the New Testament, such as God's fatherliness and the divine mercy.

Psalm 104 *Praise of God the Creator*

In this hymn the magnificence of God's creation is set forth in seven vivid scenes.

Psalm 105 *God's Fidelity to His Promise*

This psalm sings of God's fidelity in keeping His promise to Abraham, preserving His people in Egypt, bringing them back through the desert and into the Promised Land.

Psalm 106 *Israel's Confession of Sin*

This is the history of Israel, viewed as a story of continuing ingratitude, abundantly surpassed by the divine mercy.

Psalm 107 *God, the Savior of Men in Distress*

In four symbolic scenes, this psalm describes the sufferings of the time of exile and the joy of the restoration.

Psalm 108 *Prayer for Victory*

The first part of this psalm consists of a thanksgiving, which arouses trust in the mercy of God, implored in the second part.

Psalm 109 *Prayer Against a Slanderous Enemy*

Although the central section of this psalm seems to consist of a string of curses against the psalmist's enemy, it may rather represent the enemies' curses against the psalmist. If the former is true, we must bear in mind the pre-Christian milieu in which the psalms were written, a milieu in which the law of "an eye for an eye" prevailed.

Psalm 110 *The Messiah: King, Priest and Conqueror*

This is one of the most important psalms for its literal messianic character, as attested to by perennial Hebrew and Christian tradition and the teachings of Jesus Christ. Here the dignity of the Messiah is shown. He is the King appointed by God, the royal Priest, the Victor over His enemies.

Psalm 111 *Praise of God for His Goodness*

This psalm sings the power, goodness, justice and fidelity of God.

Psalm 112 *The Blessings of the Just Man*

This psalm proclaims the blessedness of those who accept God's Law and put it into practice.

Psalm 113 *Praise of the Lord for His Care of the Lowly*

This psalm is an invitation to praise God always and everywhere, because He is the Most High, the benign protector of the poor.

Psalm 114 *The Lord's Wonders at the Exodus*

This is a brief but lively commemoration of the wonders that God worked for His people during the Exodus and their entrance into the Promised Land.

Psalm 115 *The Greatness and Goodness of the True God*

This psalm seems to express a strong reaction of the Babylonian exiles against their captors' taunts that pagan deities had conquered the God of Israel.

Psalm 116 *Thanksgiving to God for Help in Need*

This psalm consists of two distinct parts—the first, a hymn of thanksgiving; the second, an expression of confidence and gratitude.

Psalm 117 *Doxology of All the Nations*

This brief psalm was probably a doxology repeated at the beginning and end of liturgical functions. The reference to all nations is important, for it shows the Israelites' consciousness of having been chosen by God for the salvation of the world.

Psalm 118 *Hymn of Thanksgiving to the Savior of Israel*

This is a solemn song of thanksgiving, probably used in processions to the Temple.

Psalm 119 *Praise of God's Law*

The longest psalm in the entire Psalter, Psalm 119 teaches the excellence of keeping God's Law.

Psalm 120 *A Complaint Against Treacherous Tongues*

This psalm is a prayer against the tongues of the wicked.

Psalm 121 *The Lord, Our Guardian*

The psalmist, who is himself confident in God's help, also reassures his companion of the Lord's protection.

Psalm 122 *The Pilgrims' Greetings to Jerusalem*

This psalm expresses the joy of the pilgrims as they arrive in the Holy City.

Psalm 123 *Israel's Prayer in Persecution*

This is a collective prayer of Israel, surrounded by hostile peoples. The circumstances correspond well to those narrated in the Book of Nehemiah.

Psalm 124 *The Lord, the Rescuer of His People*
This is a psalm of thanksgiving for deliverance from grave peril.

Psalm 125 *The Lord, the Protector of Israel*
This is a hymn of serene trust and faithfulness to the Lord.

Psalm 126 *The People's Prayer for Full Restoration*
This beautiful poem reflects the morale of the returned exiles, joyous over their liberation but anxious about the harsh trials they would have to undergo before the restoration of Judah was complete.

Psalm 127 *The Need of God's Blessing: His Gift of Sons*
This psalm consists of two short songs—the first, on the futility of all human endeavor without God; the second, on the blessing which children bring to their father.

Psalm 128 *The Happy Home of the Just Man*
This psalm, too, celebrates the blessings of family life.

Psalm 129 *Prayer for the Overthrow of Israel's Foes*
The people lament the sufferings caused by enemy nations.

Psalm 130 *Prayer for Pardon and Mercy*
This psalm is the well-known *De Profundis,* used by the Church as a prayer for the faithful departed. It is the sixth of the penitential psalms.

Psalm 131 *Humble Trust in God*
The psalmist protests his humility and simplicity and expresses the hope that Israel, too, will have a childlike trust in the Lord.

Psalm 132 *The Pact Between David and the Lord*
This psalm recalls David's concern about a dwelling place for the ark and the Lord's promise to bless the king and his dynasty.

Psalm 133 *The Benefits of Brotherly Concord*

The psalmist rejoices to see Israelite families living together in harmony and peace.

Psalm 134 *Exhortation to the Night Watch To Bless the Lord*

This short song encourages the priests and Levites on duty in the Temple to bless the Lord.

Psalm 135 *Praise of God, the Lord and Benefactor of Israel*

This psalm praises the Lord, the only true God.

Psalm 136 *Hymn of Thanksgiving for the Everlasting Kindness of the Lord*

This is a sort of litany. It was recited at Passover, after Psalms 113-118, to praise God as Creator, Deliverer, and universal Provider.

Psalm 137 *The Exile's Remembrance of Zion*

This is a sad recollection of the fall of Jerusalem to the Babylonians and the years of exile.

Psalm 138 *Hymn of a Grateful Heart*

The psalmist thanks God for listening to his prayer and expresses his wish that all the great ones of the earth may join in his hymn of gratitude.

Psalm 139 *The All-Knowing and Ever-Present God*

This is a beautiful hymn to God's infinite knowledge and power.

Psalm 140 *Prayer for Deliverance from the Snares of the Wicked*

Trusting in God's protection, the psalmist asks the Lord to rescue him from evildoers and render due justice to all.

Psalm 141 *Prayer of a Just Man To Be Saved from Wickedness*

The psalmist asks God to save him from being led astray.

Psalm 142 *Prayer of a Prisoner in Dire Straits*
The psalmist asks God to rescue him from the enemies that surround him.

Psalm 143 *Prayer of a Penitent in Distress*
In sorrow the psalmist begs God's help and guidance. This is the seventh of the penitential psalms.

Psalm 144 *Prayer for Victory and Prosperity*
The psalmist both thanks God and asks His help.

Psalm 145 *The Greatness and Goodness of God*
The psalmist exalts God's majesty, as shown in His works and His goodness towards men.

Psalm 146 *Trust in God Alone*
This psalm is a call to praise the Lord, for He alone is all powerful and good.

Psalm 147 *Zion's Grateful Praise to Her Bountiful Lord*
This psalm celebrates God, the Restorer of Israel.

Psalm 148 *Hymn of All Creation to the Almighty Creator*
Heaven and earth are invited to take part in a great concert in praise of the Lord.

Psalm 149 *Invitation To Glorify the Lord with Song and Sword*
Israel is invited to praise the Lord joyfully day and night. At the same time that they praise the Lord, they must be ready to defend His honor.

Psalm 150 *Final Doxology with Full Orchestra*
This psalm is a fitting conclusion to the entire Psalter. All creatures must form a chorus of praise to the Lord. The universe is the temple of God, and all its inhabitants must adore Him.

STUDY QUESTIONS

1. *What is the Psalter?*
2. *Name five kinds of psalms.*
3. *Are the psalms relevant today? Explain.*

The Book of Proverbs

As did all the ancient peoples, the Hebrews too had a rich patrimony of maxims for practical life. Thus, the Book of Proverbs is a compilation of various collections of short thoughts and reflections made over several centuries. They represent the wisdom of the ancient sages of Israel.

The Book of Proverbs was written in Hebrew, and even though it has many unknown authors, the main part of it is attributed to Solomon, the patron of Hebrew wisdom.

The contents cover all the different situations of real life in a practical way. Thus, men are divided into two categories: the wise and the foolish. The wise are the virtuous. The foolish are the wicked. God punishes vice and rewards virtue—truth, justice, charity, uprightness, humility, purity! The fear of the Lord is considered the source of all virtue.

The teachings in the first chapters of the Book of Proverbs are human and secular; further on they become sacred. Christ and the Apostles quoted Proverbs several times; at other times they repeated these teachings in other words. However, as with the rest of the Old Testament, Jesus' teachings in the Gospel transcended and completed the teachings of the Book of Proverbs.

The Book of Proverbs begins with a prologue on the value of Wisdom. It is interesting to note how Wisdom is presented here—not as a natural quality, but as a person. In fact, in chapter 8, Wisdom is presented as having a role to play in the work of creation, thus preparing for the doctrine of the pre-existence of the second Person of the Blessed Trinity: the divine Word, or Logos, in the Gospel of John.

The Epilogue closes the book by singing the praises of the ideal wife.

The Book of Proverbs is essentially didactic and concerns practical life.

STUDY QUESTIONS

1. What is the Book of Proverbs?
2. Why is chapter 8 of this book of particular interest?

The Book of Ecclesiastes

The title of this short book, *Ecclesiastes,* is the Greek translation of the Hebrew name *Qoheleth. Ecclesiastes* or *Qoheleth* is not a proper name, but a common noun, meaning "one who speaks in the assembly." The author wrote this book in the third or second century B.C. He calls himself "David's son and king in Jerusalem," that is, King Solomon—Israel's greatest sage. The use of this name, however, is a literary device intended to give the work a more authoritative tone. The author of *Ecclesiastes* is an unknown Palestinian teacher of popular wisdom. He is a realist who considers life as it actually is; but he lacks the clear supernatural perspective which was to be revealed by Christ.

His theme is the purpose and value of human life. But he applies his famous "vanity of vanities" to "everything under the sun." Man, he says, seeks happiness without ever finding it here below. Money and treasures, knowledge, wealth, enjoyment, love, life itself: All these things are illusory. Here on earth there is no justice, no recompense, no punishment. With death everything will end. Should man then despair and abandon his faith in God? No. The author of *Ecclesiastes* believes in God, and he says that there is a higher aspiration in man, but an aspiration that man cannot fulfill of himself. Therefore, *Ecclesiastes* concludes that man should enjoy what Divine Providence gives here and now.

This conclusion is naturalistic, since the author bases himself only on earthly realities and experiences. However, this book—*Ecclesiastes*—is of great importance in salvation history: first, because it shows that man aspires to higher, more sublime and everlasting goods; second, because it arouses in the reader hope for a future life.

In fact, considering the vanity of earthly and fleeting goods, men should abandon their avid desire for them and prepare themselves to receive the higher gifts—those belonging to another kingdom—the kingdom of heaven which God would soon introduce.

STUDY QUESTIONS

1. *What does "ecclesiastes" mean? What is its Hebrew equivalent?*
2. *To whom is this book attributed? What do we know of its real author and the time of the book's writing?*
3. *What is the main topic of the book?*
4. *In what way is this book especially useful?*

The Song of Songs

The title "Song of Songs," or "Canticle of Canticles," means "The greatest and most beautiful of all songs." In fact, in both the Old and New Testaments, there are numerous canticles. The title of the present book indicates that this sublime lyric poem is superior to all of them. Its theme is love. The language is that of love, and apparently it speaks of love between a man and a woman.

The great problem of the Song of Songs was and is that of interpretation. Should it be interpreted in a naturalistic, human way, or in a spiritual way? The Hebrews accepted it as a sacred book and so did the Church. Therefore, it cannot be considered as simply a collection of love songs, even though love is a most sublime thing and Matrimony an institution of God Himself. We must rather give to the Song of Songs an allegorical interpretation and consider its passionate language symbolically.

The two symbolic lovers are interpreted as God and humanity. Judaic tradition regards the relationship between lover and beloved in this book as that between God and Israel. Christian tradition interprets this relationship in terms of the union between Christ and His Church.

Both of these allegorical interpretations are acceptable to the majority of Catholic commentators today.

In describing the relationship between God and His people, between Christ and the Church, in terms of human love, the author follows the description made by the prophets Isaiah (5:1-7; 54:4-8), Jeremiah (2:31-32), Ezekiel (16:1-63) and in particular Hosea, who describes the covenant relationship between God and His people in terms of married love.

The Christian mystics—St. Bernard and St. John of the Cross—apply the deep meaning of the Song of Songs to our spiritual lives—to the union between Christ and the individual soul. The Lord is the Lover, they say, and the soul is the beloved.

Although the poem was attributed to Solomon because he was a writer of songs, from the vocabulary and style it can be deduced that this book was written around the end of the Babylonian Exile (538 B.C.) by an unknown author.

STUDY QUESTIONS

1. *How may the Song of Songs be interpreted?*
2. *Around what time was this book written?*

The Book of Wisdom

The Greek manuscripts call this book "the Wisdom of Solomon," but the Vulgate designates it simply as the Book of Wisdom.

The attribution to Solomon is a literary device. The true author is unknown, but his stress on everything related to Egypt suggests that he was a Jew of Alexandria. He was skilled in Greek, the language in which he wrote. The time of composition was probably the first century B.C.

In the tradition of the other wisdom writers, this Jewish sage extols Wisdom as the source of every good. Influenced by Platonic thought, he completes the work of his predecessors by proclaiming the immortality of the soul and the reward of the just in the next life.

The book consists of three parts: chapters 1 through 5, the way of Wisdom as contrasted with that of the wicked; chapters 6 through 9, true Wisdom; chapters 10 through 19, the works of Wisdom in the course of history.

The author presents Wisdom as a power that comes from God and guides people to Him. Wisdom condemns those who reject her. Although this process is silent and hidden now, the time will come when the just man will trustingly go forth to the judgment of God, while the wicked will recognize their error. The just will reign forever; the hope of the wicked will vanish (5:1-22).

Wisdom admonishes rulers (6:1-11) and reawakens in hearts the noble desire to possess her (6:12-25).

Wisdom is a gift of God (7:7), upright in her promises (7:8-10). She unveils the mystery of creation (7:15-21). She is the revelation of the beauty and radiance of God Himself (7:25—8:1). She cannot be obtained except through prayer (chapter 9).

Wisdom brought salvation to the Patriarchs, punished those who alienated themselves from her (10:1-14), saved the chosen people and destroyed their enemies (10:15-21).

God is merciful to sinners (11:17—12:22), but will hold men responsible for worshiping creatures rather than the Creator (13:1—15:19).

The author speaks of Wisdom as a person. This prepared for the revelation of the mystery of the Blessed Trinity. The section on the nature of Wisdom (7:22—8:8) foreshadows such great Christological passages of the New Testament as St. John's prologue, Colossians 1:15-16 and Hebrews 1:3.

STUDY QUESTIONS

1. *When and where is the Book of Wisdom believed to have been written?*
2. *How is Wisdom presented in this book?*
3. *What is particularly significant about the section on the nature of Wisdom (7:22—8:8)?*

The Book of Sirach or Ecclesiasticus

The Hebrew people called this book by the name of its author—Sirach, a sage who lived in Jerusalem. He wrote the book in Hebrew, probably between the years 200 and 175 B.C. The author's grandson translated it into Greek some time after 132 B.C. He also wrote the foreword, containing information about the book, the author and himself. The Latin title, Ecclesiasticus, meaning "Church book," is relatively recent. It seems to go back to St. Cyprian. Probably the book was called Ecclesiasticus because in the Church of the first centuries it was the book most used for catechetical instruction.

The author had studied the Scriptures with love and diligence, and he was so enriched by them that he felt the need to communicate what he had learned to his countrymen. His love for the Law, the Temple, divine worship and the priesthood led him to write a synthesis of revealed religion and natural wisdom. His message of love is addressed to his contemporaries to help them maintain religious faith and to have the courage to be able to live up to their own religious convictions.

The book is divided into large sections. The first could be considered an anthology of concise thoughts —moral lessons for all (chapters 1-43). The second contains praises of the heroes of Israel (44:1—50:21), and expresses the hope that they may have successors in the difficult times in which the author writes—the eve of the Maccabean revolt. A canticle of gratitude to the goodness of God closes this book (50:22—51:30), with an appeal to all to acquire true wisdom. The book gives rules for a peaceful and happy life based on an unlimited trust in God, the God who continuously intervenes with fatherly love in favor of His faithful.

Though Ecclesiasticus was not included in the Hebrew Bible after the first century A.D., nor accepted by Protestants, it has always been recognized by the Catholic Church as divinely inspired (with the exception of the foreword). After the Psalms, the Book of Sirach is the Book of the Old Testament most frequently quoted in the Christian liturgy.

STUDY QUESTIONS

1. *When, where and by whom was this book written?*
2. *What is the other name of this book and how does the name seem to have originated?*
3. *What is the aim of Sirach?*
4. *What is the first section of the book about?*
5. *What is the second section of the book about?*

The Prophets

In the biblical sense a *prophet* is one who has received a particular mission from God, has been gifted with particular charisms for this purpose, and speaks to mankind in God's name. Therefore, he is God's mouthpiece, God's interpreter, who relays God's Words to men.

Furthermore, the prophet is "one who sees"; he is the "seer." He sees what God shows him, in a divine light, as God makes him see it, whether present necessity or future event, although without arriving at full knowledge of the latter.

Mouthpiece of God, *spokesman* for God, the prophet did not present himself to the people to announce the divine will with words alone. Sometimes the teaching and prediction of an event (often calamitous), were preceded by symbolic actions, unusual or downright strange, which attracted the attention or the curiosity of the onlookers. The prophet would then explain the meaning, which remained more emphatically impressed through the spectacle of the symbolic action.

Prophetism accompanied the entire history of the Hebrew people. A prophet was the author of the "Protoevangelium" (Gn. 3:15). Noah, Abraham and Moses were prophets. God selected the prophet with one of His positive *calls,* or prophetical vocations (Ex. 3:10; 4:12; 1 Sm. 1:3; 1 Kgs. 19:15-21; Is. 6). For example, the Lord said to Jeremiah:

"Before I formed you in the womb I knew you,
 before you were born I dedicated you,
 a prophet to the nations I appointed you....

Say not, 'I am too young.'
To whomever I send you, you shall go;
whatever I command you, you shall speak" (Jer. 1:5-7).

The prophetic vocation depended solely upon the free will of God, without any regard for personal merits, social conditions, culture, sex or age. It was God who freely chose whom He wished. Isaiah was a nobleman; Jeremiah and Ezekiel, priests; Samuel, a Levite; Elisha, a farmer; Moses and Amos, shepherds; Abraham, a former idolater; Balaam, a pagan enemy of Israel; Miriam and Deborah, women.

Special charismatic gifts made the divine vocation of the prophet certain, so that he could speak with the authority of God, who often confirmed the prophet's mission with miracles.

The official proclamation of prophetism is delivered through Moses. In Deuteronomy (18:18-22), we have, as it were, the "constitution" of prophetism, every expression of which is an article: "I will raise up for them a prophet like you from among their brethren, and will put my words in his mouth, and he shall speak to them all that I command him. And whoever will not give heed to my words which he shall speak in my name, I myself will require it of him. But the prophet who presumes to speak a word in my name which I have not commanded him to speak, or who speaks in the name of other gods, that same prophet shall die.' And if you say in your heart, 'How may we know the word which the Lord has not spoken?'—when a prophet speaks in the name of the Lord, if the word does not come to pass or come true, that is a word which the Lord has not spoken; the prophet has spoken it presumptuously, you need not be afraid of him" (18:18-22).

Therefore, the *prophet* of Israel is distinct from the *diviner* (soothsayer or fortune-teller), from the *false prophet*, from the *prophet of idols*. Signs are indicated by which the authentic prophet is to be recognized. Furthermore, in the true prophet we have the *type* of the perfect prophet which Christ would realize fully, as St. Peter affirms in the Acts (3:20-22): "Thus may a season of refreshment be granted you by the Lord when he sends you Jesus, already designated as your Messiah. Jesus must remain in heaven until the time of universal restoration which God spoke of long ago through his holy prophets. For Moses said:

" 'The Lord God will raise up for you a prophet like me from among your own kinsmen: you shall listen to him in everything he says to you.' "

The prophets are divided into two groups: *prophets of action* and *writing prophets*. The prophets of *action* belonged to the primitive period of the history of Israel. In this primitive period of prophetism, the divine message to be communicated to men was expressed more with the actions of the life of the prophet than with his words. Therefore, the message ordinarily was brief, a simple oracle, a concise sentence, shouted to the crowd during an assembly at the gates of the city, or at the outskirts of the Temple. The primitive conciseness slowly disappeared, giving place in the later prophets to more elaborate discourses.

The following were prophets of action: Abraham; Moses; the seventy elders; Miriam, sister of Moses; Joshua; Deborah; Samuel; Nathan; Ahijah; Shemaiah; Jehu; Hanani; Jehu, son of Hanani; Jahaziel; Eliezer; Elijah; Elisha, and the disciples of the prophets.

The following were *writing* prophets: Amos, Hosea, Isaiah, Micah, Zephaniah, Jeremiah, Nahum, Habakkuk, Ezekiel, Haggai, Joel, Zechariah, Obadiah and Malachi.

It is customary to distinguish the *major prophets:* Isaiah, Jeremiah, Ezekiel, and Daniel, from the *minor prophets:* Hosea, Joel, Amos, Obadiah, Jonah, Micah, Nahum, Habakkuk, Zephaniah, Haggai, Zechariah and Malachi. This distinction is based solely upon the length of these books.

We must not forget that the Hebrews were the *people of God,* chosen by Him from among all others in such a way that they would be particularly *His:* a theocratic people, therefore—wholly dependent upon God in being and in actions.

In fact, in following the history of the chosen people, we see that it was always God who intervened to form and to guide His people, He Himself selecting His representatives, who spoke and acted *when* and *where* He wished.

He called, for example, leaders who would represent Him, such as Moses, Joshua, the Judges. And when at a certain point in Israel's history monarchy was established, at first it was still God who selected His king: He chose Saul and then David. But when the monarchy priesthood became hereditary, God selected with greater frequency these extraordinary persons—the prophets—who always intervened in the decisive moments of His people.

Thus, God continued to lead His people, at times even against the kings and the priests, who often were severely reprimanded and punished.

The prophet, therefore, was the *faithful servant* of the Word and of the will of God, faithful to Him at any cost, interpreter of the signs of the times, because he did not live outside history. He was the *voice of God,* incisive and dramatic, which unmasked sin with tremendous audacity and defended the rights of God with power and extraordinary constancy. The prophet was also the spiritual guide of the people, to whom he constantly indicated the will of God and their own good. His greatest preoccupation was to keep Israel faithful to the God of the promise, the God of salvation. He was the sentinel to keep the people alert to every danger of infidelity to the covenant (cf. Ez. 3:17; Is. 21:6-8; Hos. 9:8). Faithfulness to the covenant signified blessing, well-being, indefinite prosperity. Unfaithfulness, instead, meant punishment, invasion, destruction, exile.

It was within this framework that the prophet also spoke of the future.

After the exile, prophecy gradually disappeared from Israel. With the reforms of Ezra and Nehemiah, the foundations were laid for a substantial spiritual rebirth. In that era the prophetic preaching was followed by the collecting, editing and completing of the Sacred Books, upon which the wise men of Israel reflected and meditated, nourishing themselves and the faithful remnant with the pure font of the written Word of God.

Both the writing prophets and the prophets of action were first of all preachers, announcers of the Word of God. In general, they only wrote down excerpts of their preaching. Then, after a period of oral transmission, more or less lengthy, the listeners or disciples of the "writing" prophets, faithful to the original thought and to the oral traditions which had transmitted it, gave us the present prophetic books. Since the period of preaching lasted several years in certain cases, such as that of Isaiah, we find various topics following each other without any connection.

All the prophets had in common the substance of their message, that is, as messengers of God they made known His manner of dealing with men and His designs for fulfilling His plan of salvation. They were also the principal organs of the progress of revelation. Thus we find in them *monotheism,* insofar as all the prophets applied themselves to keeping the Hebrew people rooted in faith in one God and in fidelity to the covenant made with Him. Besides this, the prophets presented God as the Master and Lord of all the other peoples; as the One who was holy and most careful of the welfare of His people.

In relation to the holiness of God, the prophets expressed *morality,* insofar as they became aware of sin and fought against it under every aspect. To avoid sin they fostered a religion which was not only exterior, but first of all interior, that is, it consisted in the practice of the Decalogue in its entirety.

But the prophets did not stop at threats provoked by the infidelity of the chosen people. They spoke of the plan of salvation, of the *Messiah* who would establish the kingdom of God. The Messiah would be a descendant of David (2 Sm. 7:13ff.), a shepherd (Ez. 34:23f.), a humble ruler (Zec. 9:9), who would give His life for the salvation of the people (Is. 42:1-7; 49:1-9; 50:4-9;

52:13—53:12). He would be born of a virgin (Is. 7:14) in Bethlehem of Judea (Mi. 5:1-2).

Thus, the prophetic books formed part of the precious heritage of Israel. They were read and meditated by each new generation, who learned from them their strong spirit of faith.

STUDY QUESTIONS

1. *Explain the prophet as "seer" and "God's mouthpiece."*
2. *Could anyone become a prophet in Israel? Explain.*
3. *How could a genuine prophet be identified?*
4. *How, in general, did the earlier prophets in Israel differ from the later prophets?*
5. *What was the prophet's chief concern?*
6. *When did prophecy disappear and what replaced it?*
7. *How did the prophets present God? morality? the Messiah?*

The Book of Isaiah

Isaiah occupies the first place in the canon of the prophets because of the importance of his prophecies, the amplitude of his work and the sublimity of his style.

Born around the year 765 B.C., he belonged to a noble family and lived in Jerusalem. He married through divine command and had at least two sons, to whom he gave symbolic names. He began his prophetic mission in Jerusalem and carried it out in the southern kingdom, Judah.

After the Assyrian invasion in 701, Isaiah disappeared from the political scene. Tradition says that sometime during the reign of the impious king, Manasseh (693-639), he was put to death by being sawed in half.

The times in which Isaiah performed his prophetic ministry were certainly not favorable for a spiritual renewal. Together with political instability, caused by the Assyrian expansion, moral corruption was widespread. Superstitious concepts, pagan customs, immorality, social injustices, drunkenness, and immoderate ambition constituted the order of the day. The worship given to God in the Temple was more formalistic than heartfelt, and the faith was languishing, showing itself incapable of sustaining a life worthy of the people which God had chosen for His inheritance.

In such an environment Isaiah announced his message, severely castigating individual and collective faults, reproving and threatening. But he especially sought to inculcate an unlimited trust in God, as support, guide and savior.

The Book of Isaiah consists of sixty-six chapters. It is usually divided into two great parts, the first of which is called the Book of the Judgments of God (chapters 1-39), and the second the Book of Consolation (chapters 40-66).

The importance of the Book of Isaiah is extraordinary. It not only employs classical Hebrew and a generally elevated style, but also details a most delicate period in the civil and religious history of the kingdom of Judah. Yet its importance is especially based on its numerous and very clear prophecies regarding the future Messiah. These merited for it the title "Protoevangelium" (anticipated Gospel). The principal messianic texts are those regarding the virginal conception and birth of the Messiah (7:14); His divinity and humanity (9:6); His descent from the house of David (11:1, 10); and His expiatory passion and death (chapter 53).

The first part of the Book of Isaiah comprises oracles concerning Judah and Jerusalem (chapters 1-6); the Book of Emmanuel (chapters 7-12); oracles against the nations (chapters 13-23); eschatological oracles, or great apocalypses (chapters 24-27); the six woes (chapters 28-33); the little apocalypse (chapters 34-35); an historical appendix (chapters 36-39).

The second part comprises oracles regarding the liberation from the Exile (40-48); the messianic liberation (49-55); the return of the captives (56-66). In this second part are found the famous "songs of the servant of God" (cf. chapters 42, 49, 50, 52, 53). He suffers to pay for our sins, but God exalts him in the end. In the servant songs the early Christian Church and Patristic exegesis see the passion, death and resurrection of Jesus.

Only with great difficulty can one attribute the whole work to one sole author, because of the difference in historical background of the major parts of the book. Thus, by almost unanimous accord, the first part of the book—chapters 1 through 39—is attributed to the historical Isaiah, whereas chapters 40 through 55 are ascribed to an anonymous author, probably a disciple of the Isaian school, who lived in Babylon toward the end of the Exile, and chapters 56 through 66 are thought to be the work of another author, who lived in Palestine among the returned exiles. Naturally, all the authors were inspired. The collection of the various writings took place at the beginning of the third century B.C.

Isaiah is called the prophet of faith, because he demands absolute faith and abandonment in God, rather than any trust in human powers. He is called the prophet of God's holiness, because of the incomparable transcendence of God, whom he describes as the thrice-holy One (6:3). Furthermore, he can be called the *messianic* prophet because of his oracles about the ideal king (chapters 6-12), the cornerstone of the new kingdom (28:16-17), who will be the principal agent of a salvation which will be universal (42:1-53). In Jesus Christ these messianic prophecies are fulfilled.

STUDY QUESTIONS

1. *Who was Isaiah and when did he live?*
2. *Why is the Book of Isaiah placed first among the prophetical books?*
3. *Describe the period in which the first part of Isaiah was written.*
4. *What does the Book of Isaiah tell about the Messiah?*
5. *What is the common opinion about the authorship of this book?*

The Book of Jeremiah

Jeremiah lived a century after Isaiah. He was born around the year 650 B.C., of a priestly family living near the city of Jerusalem. He received his prophetic vocation about the year 626 B.C., when he was a little over twenty years of age. By order of the Lord, Jeremiah did not marry.

He was sensitive, a man of peace, and yet God gave him a mission he could not refuse: Jeremiah lived through the critical years which preceded and succeeded the destruction of the kingdom of Judah, because of sin. The tender-hearted prophet had to proclaim a message which was opposed to the Temple of God, His city and His people.

A prophet of doom, he had to announce catastrophic events. Because of this he was persecuted, imprisoned, threatened and eventually put to death. But he never abandoned his mission; he was a true type of the divine, patient Jesus, who was likewise persecuted and put to death by "His own," whose salvation He sought.

Jeremiah was a messianic prophet, not so much in his writings—in fact, his messianic prophecies are few—but rather because in his own life he more than any other prophet resembled the Messiah.

The ministry of Jeremiah lasted about forty years. From chapter 36 of his book, we know that he dictated to his disciple, Baruch, all the words that Yahweh had spoken to him about Jerusalem, Judah and the nations. However, this first collection was destroyed by the king of Judah. It was replaced by another one, as we read in 36:32: "Jeremiah took another scroll, and gave it to his secretary, Baruch...; he wrote on it at Jeremiah's dictation all the words contained in the book which

Jehoiakim, king of Judah, had burned in the fire, and many others of the same kind in addition."

The Book of Jeremiah is divided into two sections. The first contains the oracles against Judah and Jerusalem (chapters 1-45). It relates these in a non-chronological order, together with many historical narratives.

The second section (chapters 46-51) contains the oracles against the pagan nations, followed by a brief historical appendix (chapter 52).

Because of his writings, Jeremiah is among the prophets whose spiritual life and interior sentiments are best known.

This prophet cries over the ingratitude of the princes of Judah, the priests, and the people, who added infidelity to infidelity toward God, thus calling down punishments upon themselves as well as the privation of what God had promised them—land, Temple and descendants. But he also sees a future restoration in a new covenant:

"This is the covenant which I will make with the house of Israel after those days, says the Lord: I will put my law within them, and I will write it upon their hearts; and I will be their God, and they shall be my people. And no longer shall each man teach his neighbor and each his brother, saying, 'Know the Lord,' for they shall all know me, from the least of them to the greatest, says the Lord; for I will forgive their iniquity, and I will remember their sin no more" (31:33-34).

STUDY QUESTIONS

1. *How does Jeremiah's mission contrast with his temperament?*
2. *Chiefly, in what way is Jeremiah a messianic prophet?*
3. *What is the composition of the Book of Jeremiah?*
4. *Is Jeremiah only a prophet of doom? Explain.*

The Book of Lamentations

These five short poems, placed immediately after the Book of Jeremiah, are entitled in the Greek Bible, or Septuagint, and in the Vulgate (but not in the Hebrew Bible), the "Lamentations of Jeremiah," because the subject matter reflects the times of the prophet.

The Lamentations were written in Palestine after the fall of Jerusalem in 587, and were probably chanted by the Jews in the synagogue on the occasion of the anniversary of this tragic event. It was, therefore, for a liturgical reason that the Lamentations were detached from the prophetical books.

The Lamentations are not a hymn of desperation; while the author (or authors) describes the mourning of the people over the punishment due to their sins, he also shows their whole-hearted repentance and implores God's mercy and forgiveness.

For a long time the Book of Lamentations was attributed to Jeremiah. Today there is the tendency to admit his hand in the second, third, and fourth poems, but to see the hand of another in the first and fifth.

STUDY QUESTIONS

1. What are the Lamentations and what, probably, was their original use?
2. Where are the Lamentations positioned in the Bible? Why is this placement appropriate?

The Book of Baruch

This small book gives us important information about the Jewish community during their exile in Babylon. It contains five very different compositions:
1) an historical introduction
2) a confession of sins and a prayer of the exiles
3) praise of Wisdom identified with the Law of Moses
4) a prophetic passage: Jerusalem is assured that her captive children will be restored to her
5) the Letter of Jeremiah against idolatry.

The book was not written by Baruch himself, at least not entirely. To him, probably, can be attributed the first part, which totally reflects the thought and style of Jeremiah. The rest was written either in the second or first century. Even the Letter of Jeremiah is the work of an unknown author, who, however, must have been a witness of the Babylonian cult.

The original Book of Baruch, written in Hebrew, is now lost.

Because the Jews—at least those who decided upon the actual canon of the present Hebrew Bible—did not consider it a sacred book, the Book of Baruch is among the deuterocanonical books. It is contained, however, in the Greek Bible, or Septuagint, as well as in the Vulgate. The Catholic Church has always considered the Book of Baruch as sacred and inspired.

STUDY QUESTIONS

1. *With what period does the Book of Baruch appear to be concerned?*
2. *Who was Baruch? How much of this book may be attributed to him?*

The Book of Ezekiel

Like Jeremiah, Ezekiel, too, was a priest. He was deported to Babylon with many other members of the Jewish community in 597 B.C. In 593, after five years in exile, at the age of about thirty (1:1), he began his prophetic ministry, which lasted at least twenty-two years (29:17). He was the moral leader of the captives and died in exile—probably killed by a prince of Judah whom he had reprimanded for his idolatry.

The Book of Ezekiel is centered on the fall of Jerusalem. Before the fall of the Holy City, Ezekiel's prophecies aimed at exhorting the people to repent and trust in God. He insisted that Babylon would triumph and the kingdom of Judah would fall.

After the fall of Jerusalem, his prophecies were intended to console the exiles with promises of liberation, of the return to their own land, and of the messianic kingdom. However, his mission was very difficult, because the exiles, instead of listening to him, turned away from Yahweh and fell into idolatry.

The Book of Ezekiel can be divided into two large sections. It begins with a prologue which describes the vision of the chariot of Yahweh and the vocation of the prophet (chapters 1-3).

The first main part (chapters 4-32) regards prophecies of impending divine punishment for the people of God because of their sins. To the exiles he foretells that even the Temple will be destroyed. However, this destruction will not be final.

In the second part (chapters 33-48), after having announced the ruin of Jerusalem, Ezekiel prophesies a material and messianic restoration. The new covenant and new kingdom will call for a new heart and new spirit in each person. This is to be accomplished through the assistance of God.

Thus Ezekiel helped to pave the way for the doctrine of grace leading to salvation which would be clearly revealed in the New Testament.

To express future events, Ezekiel abundantly uses symbolic actions. For this reason the prophet is sometimes obscure. He performs acts symbolic of the siege of Jerusalem (chapters 4-5), the departure of the exiles (12:1-7), etc.

Ezekiel is a visionary. Four formal visions occupy a substantial part of the book. Among them is the famous vision of the dry bones (chapter 37). This expresses the rising of Israel from the graveyard of Babylon to a new life.

Ezekiel is the prophet of the glory of God. In the Book of Ezekiel, God manifests Himself in His majesty. The concept of the love of God very seldom appears in this prophet's vocabulary.

An important point in the Book of Ezekiel is the placing of responsibility for sin on the individual. This doctrine marks a step forward in Hebrew theology, which until then believed in collective retribution: "The word of the Lord came to me again: 'What do you mean by repeating this proverb concerning the land of Israel, "The fathers have eaten sour grapes, and the children's teeth are set on edge"? As I live, says the Lord God, this proverb shall no more be used by you in Israel. Behold, all souls are mine; the soul of the father as well as the soul of the son is mine: the soul that sins shall die'" (18:1-4).

Ezekiel has his messianic hopes as do the other prophets. He speaks about the Messiah and says that He is to be a new David, a "shepherd" of His people (34:23; 37:24); and a ruler (34:24) who will pasture His sheep along ways of peace and security.

STUDY QUESTIONS

1. When and where did Ezekiel begin to prophesy?
2. Around what central event do Ezekiel's prophecies revolve? What sort of a shift do they undergo when that event has actually taken place?
3. What is noteworthy about the way in which God's message comes to Ezekiel? About the manner in which he often transmits it?
4. Name some important points in Ezekiel's content.

The Book of Daniel

The Book of Daniel takes its name not from the author, who is unknown, but from its hero. Daniel was a young Jew deported to Babylon about 605 B.C. There he was chosen for the service of Nebuchadnezzar and given the name of Belteshazzar. He was handsome, intelligent and wise, with an extraordinary ability to interpret dreams. (This Daniel is not to be confused with the Daniel of Ezekiel—Ez. 14:14.)

The Book of Daniel contains popular traditions about him and his three companions. These four characters are not purely legendary; the stories rest on older historical tradition. The book also contains more recent additions of the second century B.C., when the definitive composition was completed. It was written to comfort and to sustain the faith and hope of the Jewish people during the persecution of Antiochus IV Epiphanes. Thus the persecuted Jews of the second century B.C. could find in the lives of the persecuted Daniel and his companions application to their own lives. Also, as Daniel and his companions emerged victorious from their trials, so would the Jews. And as Daniel's persecutors were forced to acknowledge the power of the true God, so the contemporary persecutor (Antiochus Epiphanes) would suffer the wrath of Yahweh.

In the Book of Daniel there are visions. These have the same purpose as the opening narratives: to reveal the mystery of the future salvation, when the persecutors will be conquered and the kingdom of God and His saints will arrive (2:44; 7:18, 25, 27).

The prophecy contained in the Book of Daniel could be considered as a point of arrival in God's intervention in all preceding history as well as in the history of the future. The kingdom of God will be extended to all nations (7:14); it will be God's kingdom (4:31), the kingdom of saints (7:18), the kingdom of the "Son of Man"—the Messiah—to whom all dominion is given (7:13-14).

Written in an apocalyptic style, this book represents a mature Old Testament use of this literary form. Its counterpart in the New Testament is the Book of Revelation, in which the persecuted Church looks with trust to the coming of her Head and King (Rv. 22:20).

The Book of Daniel has come to us in three different languages: Hebrew, Aramaic and Greek. This last one contains so-called "deuterocanonical" sections—those not found in the Hebrew canon (3:26-45, 52-90; 13:1-14, 42) —inspired, however, as is the rest of the Bible.

STUDY QUESTIONS

1. *When and why was the Book of Daniel written?*
2. *Who was Daniel and when did he live?*
3. *What are some of the prophecies that the Book of Daniel contains?*
4. *What is the literary form of the book?*

The Book of Hosea

Hosea belonged to the Northern Kingdom and he probably lived to see the fall of Samaria in the year 721 B.C. His prophetic ministry lasted for a period of about forty years.

Hosea's book is certainly only a summary of his activity, as is true with all the minor prophets.

Of Hosea's life during his turbulent times we know nothing beyond what he himself narrates about his matrimonial troubles (chapters 1-3). The prophet's sad marital experience profoundly influences his teachings.

Hosea has married a wife, Gomer, whom he loves but who deserts him. His love for her remains, however, and after trying her, he takes her back. Gomer, the adulteress, symbolizes faithless Israel, the bride of God, whose infidelity has taken the form of idolatry and cruel oppression of the poor. But God's love for her remains. And thus the theme of the Book of Hosea is God's love for Israel as a spouse. Yahweh will punish her, but only to save her and bring her back to the joys of her first love and happiness.

Hosea is the first prophet who expresses the relations between Yahweh and Israel in terms of marriage. The wedding symbolism of God's love for His people is imitated later on in the Old Testament, especially in the Song of Songs. In the New Testamemt, both St. John and St. Paul apply it to the union between Christ and His Church. Christian mysticism extends it also to the union between Christ and the individual soul.

STUDY QUESTIONS

1. *How does Hosea use the image of marriage to express God's message?*
2. *How has this image been extended in later writings?*

The Book of Joel

It is believed that this prophet exercised his ministry in Judea about 400 B.C. The main theme of the Book of Joel is the day of the Lord.

This book begins with a terrible invasion of locusts in the land of Judah. The prophet invites the people to penance and prayer. To this Yahweh replies by promising the cessation of the plague and an abundance of graces (2:27). The fullness of this grace is to come at the time of the Messiah.

Joel's contribution is to prophesy the outpouring of the Spirit on all God's people in the messianic age (3:1-5). This is a clear announcement of the beginnings of the Church, since the effusion of the Holy Spirit on the day of Pentecost is interpreted and explained by St. Peter as the fulfillment of the promise of Joel (Acts 2:16-21).

STUDY QUESTIONS

1. *What is the main theme of the Book of Joel?*
2. *What is the significance of this book in regard to the New Testament?*

The Book of Amos

Amos was a shepherd of Tekoa in Judah (1:1). He was sent by God to prophesy to the Northern Kingdom of Israel. Amos remained there only for a brief time, because the priest in charge of the schismatic royal sanctuary at Bethel forced him to leave.

The prophet preached during the prosperous reign of Jeroboam II (783-743 B.C.). He denounced social injustice, the hypocrisy of a religion that was purely exterior, and infidelity to God (5:21-22).

The punishment of God is ever present in the prophet's mind (1; 2; 6:8-9, 14). But he also speaks of the salvation of those who remain faithful to the demands of Yahweh (5:15).

STUDY QUESTIONS

1. *Who was Amos and when did he prophesy?*
2. *What evils, especially, did Amos denounce?*

The Book of Obadiah

Nothing is known of this prophet. His book is the shortest in the Old Testament (21 verses), and it was perhaps written sometime in the 5th century B.C.

Obadiah announces the vengeance of Yahweh against Edom, a longstanding enemy of the people of God. He also concludes with a promise of salvation for the chosen people.

STUDY QUESTIONS

1. *What is the Book of Obadiah about?*
2. *When may this book have been written?*

The Book of Jonah

Unlike the other prophetic books, this short work is a parable to teach true religion. It was written after the Exile, sometime in the 5th century B.C.

Jonah, the hero of this partly humorous adventure, is a reluctant, complaining prophet who, upon seeing the repentance of the Ninevites, the enemies of Israel, is upset because God does not carry out the punishment He has threatened.

A very sublime lesson is to be derived from this narrative—God's love and mercy are universal.

The Book of Jonah is a didactic narrative. And Jesus Himself uses this Old Testament story as Christian preachers use the New Testament parables.

STUDY QUESTIONS

1. What is the message of the Book of Jonah?
2. About when was this book written?

The Book of Micah

Micah is one of the ancient prophets, a contemporary of Isaiah.

Of his life and call we know nothing, except that he came from an obscure village of Judea. He prophesied in the kingdom of Judah between the 8th and 7th centuries B.C. The prophet fearlessly announced God's message of condemnation (1:2; 6:1-2), because of corruption in religion and especially in morals. He reproaches the greedy capitalists, the usurers, the tyrants, the families divided by rivalry. But the prophet speaks also of hope (7:7). He affirms that a remnant will survive the chastisement of Judah (4:7).

In the New Testament, the scribes consulted by King Herod quote the passage of Micah (5:2) as a prophecy foretelling that Bethlehem will be the Messiah's birthplace (Mt. 2:3-6).

STUDY QUESTIONS

1. *Where did Micah come from and when did he prophesy?*
2. *What messianic prophecy do we find in Micah?*

The Book of Nahum

Nahum is a contemporary of Jeremiah. The Book of Nahum opens with a prophecy contrasting the punishment of Assyria with the restoration of Judah (1:2—2:3).

This book vibrates with the joy of Israel over the forthcoming rapid ruin of Assyria (612 B.C.), her traditional oppressor. But that joy was to last only a short time because the fall of Jerusalem, too, would soon follow.

STUDY QUESTIONS

1. *When was the Book of Nahum written?*
2. *What is the theme of this book?*

The Book of Habakkuk

Habakkuk was a contemporary of Jeremiah. He prophesied from the year 605 to 597 B.C. He maintains, as Jeremiah does, that Nebuchadnezzar is an instrument in the hands of God to punish His unfaithful people.

In the first two chapters Habakkuk dialogues with God and boldly questions the Lord about the way He governs the world. Almighty God answers him that He will save those who are faithful to Him, those who trust in Him:

"The rash man" says the Lord, "has no integrity;
  but the just man, because of his faith, shall live" (2:4).

This is a precious maxim, which will be quoted in the letters to the Romans (1:17), Galatians (3:11), and Hebrews (10:38).

The third chapter is a magnificent prayer of confidence in which the prophet implores Yahweh for deliverance.

STUDY QUESTIONS

1. *What are the first two chapters of the Book of Habakkuk about?*
2. *In what does the third chapter consist?*

The Book of Zephaniah

We know nothing about Zephaniah except that he was of royal descent and that he prophesied between 640 and 609 B.C.

In chapter 1, the prophet harshly protests against the religious degradation of Judah and Jerusalem, announcing the impending punishment of God, presented as the day of the Lord, a day of disaster (1:2-18).

In chapter 2, the prophet presents the day of the Lord as a day of judgment for the enemies of God's people.

In chapter 3, Zephaniah still reproaches Jerusalem, which accepts no correction. But he, too, speaks of a remnant,

"a people humble and lowly,
Who shall take refuge in the name of the Lord:
 the remnant of Israel" (3:12-13).

The final message is one of joy. It foretells the messianic times of restoration and peace (3:14-20).

STUDY QUESTIONS

1. *Where and at what time did Zephaniah prophesy?*
2. *What themes, familiar from earlier prophets, are found again in Zephaniah?*

The Book of Haggai

Haggai exercised his prophetic ministry in the post-exilic period, in the year 520 B.C. The prophet stirs up the spirits of the discouraged Jews who have returned from Babylon. He urges them to bring to completion the rebuilding of the Temple, recalling the promises that the ancient prophets linked with this edifice.

As construction proceeds, Haggai jubilantly announces that this Temple will indeed afford a pledge of the glory which God will one day reveal to His people.

STUDY QUESTIONS

1. *When and where did Haggai prophesy?*
2. *What was Haggai's message?*

The Book of Zechariah

Zechariah was a contemporary of Haggai, and like him he exercised the prophetic ministry among the Jews who had returned to Jerusalem from the Babylonian Exile.

St. Jerome used to call the Book of Zechariah obscure. In reality, it is such because of the difficulty involved in learning the true meaning of the many symbols, as well as the scarcity of historical facts about the times of the prophet.

This book can be divided into three parts. The first, chapters 1 through 6, contains symbolic visions. The second, chapters 7 through 8, inculcates the preference to be given to interior spiritual dispositions over external observances. The third, chapters 9 through 14, is entirely different in style and content, and seems to have been written by a prophet of the 4th century B.C. It is, however, of particular interest because of its messianic references. In fact, the New Testament applies to the life of Jesus various passages of this section: for example, the triumphal entrance of Jesus into Jerusalem as a humble and gentle Messiah (Mt. 21:4-5; Zec. 9:9), the killing of the shepherd and the scattering of the flock (Mt. 26:31; Zec. 13:7), and the recognition of the "pierced" Messiah (Jn. 19:37; Zec. 12:10).

STUDY QUESTIONS

1. *When did Zechariah prophesy?*
2. *In what century is the last part of this book believed to have been written?*
3. *What makes the first part of the Book of Zechariah obscure?*
4. *Why is the last part of this book of particular interest to Christians?*

The Book of Malachi

The author of this book is probably anonymous. It seems that his name is taken from chapter 3, verse 1, where the word "Malachi" means, "my messenger." The book was composed in the 5th century B.C., after the Jewish community had returned from Babylon.

The prophet stresses two themes. The first is the failure of priests (1:6; 2:9) and of people (3:6-12) in their religious duties, as well as the scandal of mixed marriage and divorce (2:10-16). These he condemns.

As the second theme, the prophet foretells the coming of God Himself, who will purify all things and bring about the triumph of the virtuous (3:1-5, 13-21). God's precursor will be Elijah. (The New Testament declares that John the Baptist, the precursor of Jesus, came with the spirit and the power of Elijah—Lk. 1:17.)

Most important of all in the Book of Malachi is 1:11, a prophecy that a pure oblation will be offered to the Lord from all the earth, to replace the ancient, impure sacrifices. This announcement has been traditionally interpreted as a foretelling of the unique Sacrifice of the Mass, a perfect Sacrifice offered to God in all the nations.

STUDY QUESTIONS

1. *Do we know the name of the author of the Book of Malachi? Explain.*
2. *When was the Book of Malachi written?*
3. *What is the prophet's first theme? What is his concluding theme?*
4. *What famous prophecy is found in chapter 1?*

THE TEMPLE OF JERUSALEM

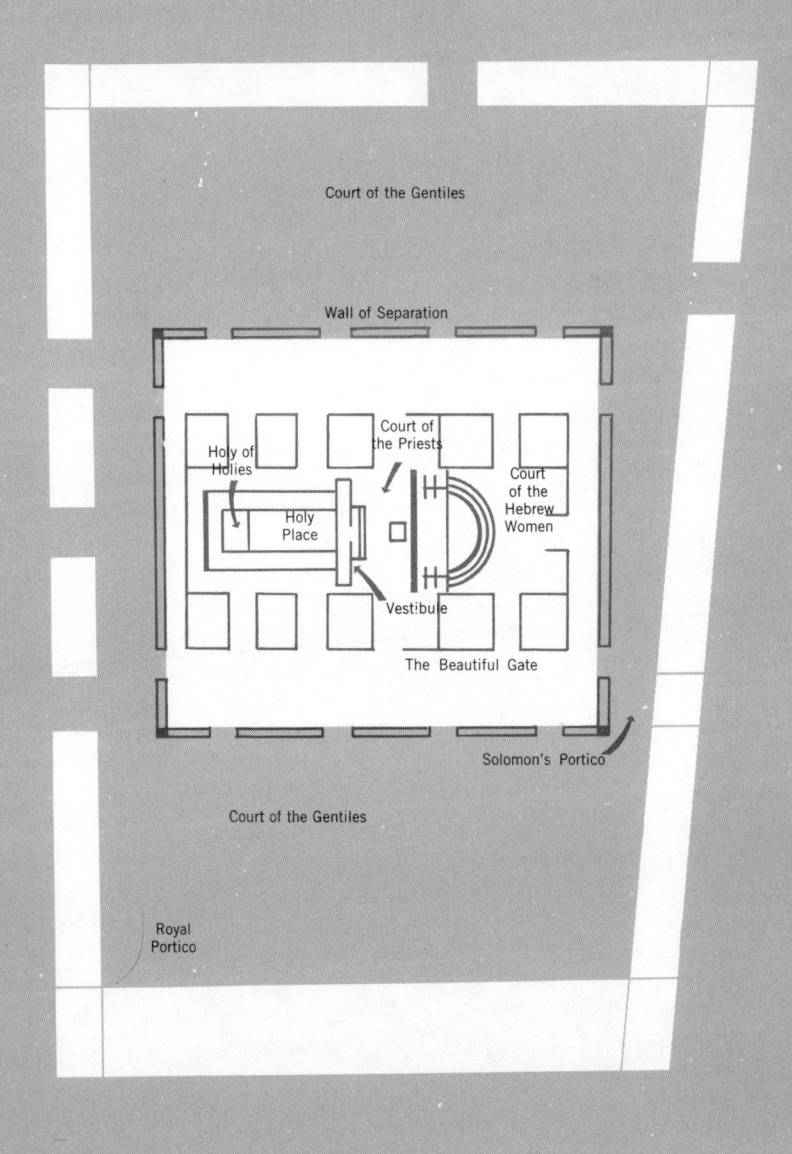

Court of the Gentiles

Wall of Separation

Holy of Holies

Court of the Priests

Holy Place

Court of the Hebrew Women

Vestibule

The Beautiful Gate

Solomon's Portico

Court of the Gentiles

Royal Portico

The New Testament

THE GEOGRAPHY OF THE HOLY LAND

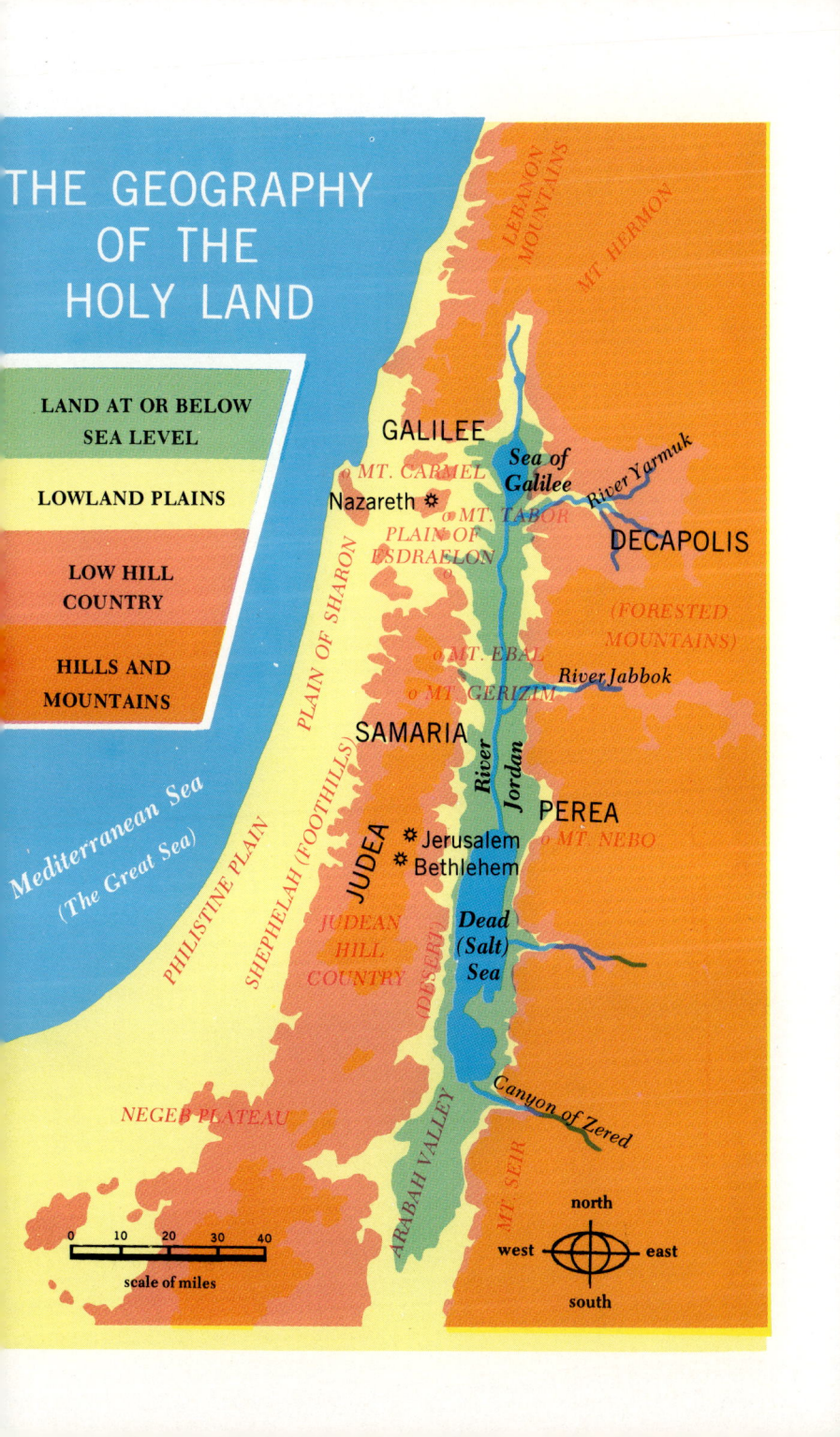

LAND AT OR BELOW SEA LEVEL

LOWLAND PLAINS

LOW HILL COUNTRY

HILLS AND MOUNTAINS

LEBANON MOUNTAINS
MT. HERMON
GALILEE
MT. CARMEL
Sea of Galilee
Nazareth
MT. TABOR
River Yarmuk
PLAIN OF ESDRAELON
DECAPOLIS
PLAIN OF SHARON
(FORESTED MOUNTAINS)
MT. EBAL
River Jabbok
MT. GERIZIM
SAMARIA
Mediterranean Sea (The Great Sea)
SHEPHELAH (FOOTHILLS)
River Jordan
PEREA
PHILISTINE PLAIN
JUDEA
Jerusalem
Bethlehem
MT. NEBO
JUDEAN HILL COUNTRY
(DESERT)
Dead (Salt) Sea
NEGEB PLATEAU
ARABAH VALLEY
Canyon of Zered
MT. SEIR

north / west / east / south

0 10 20 30 40
scale of miles

Journey of Abraham (about 1850 B.C.)

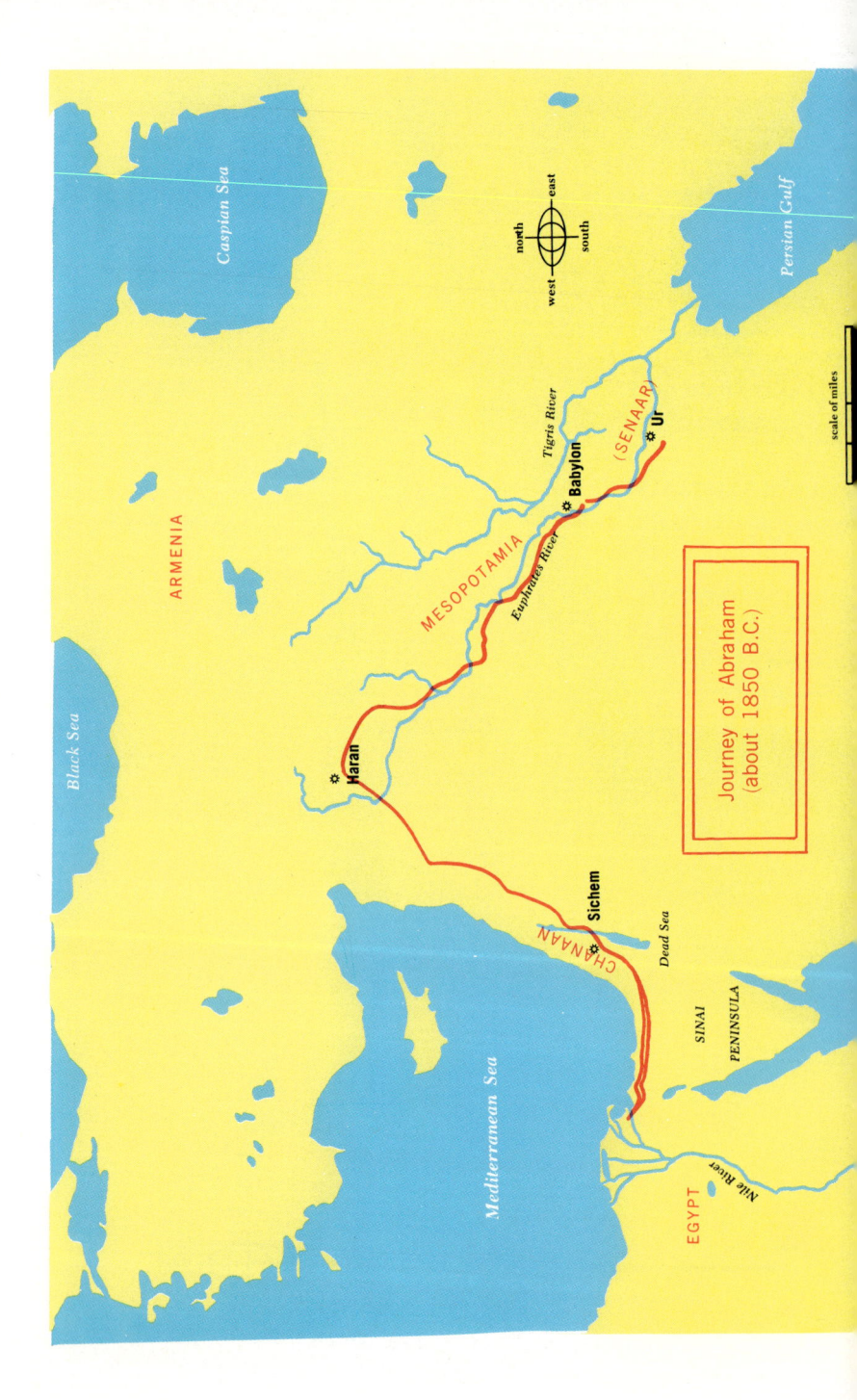

POSSIBLE ROUTE OF THE ISRAELITES TO CHANAAN

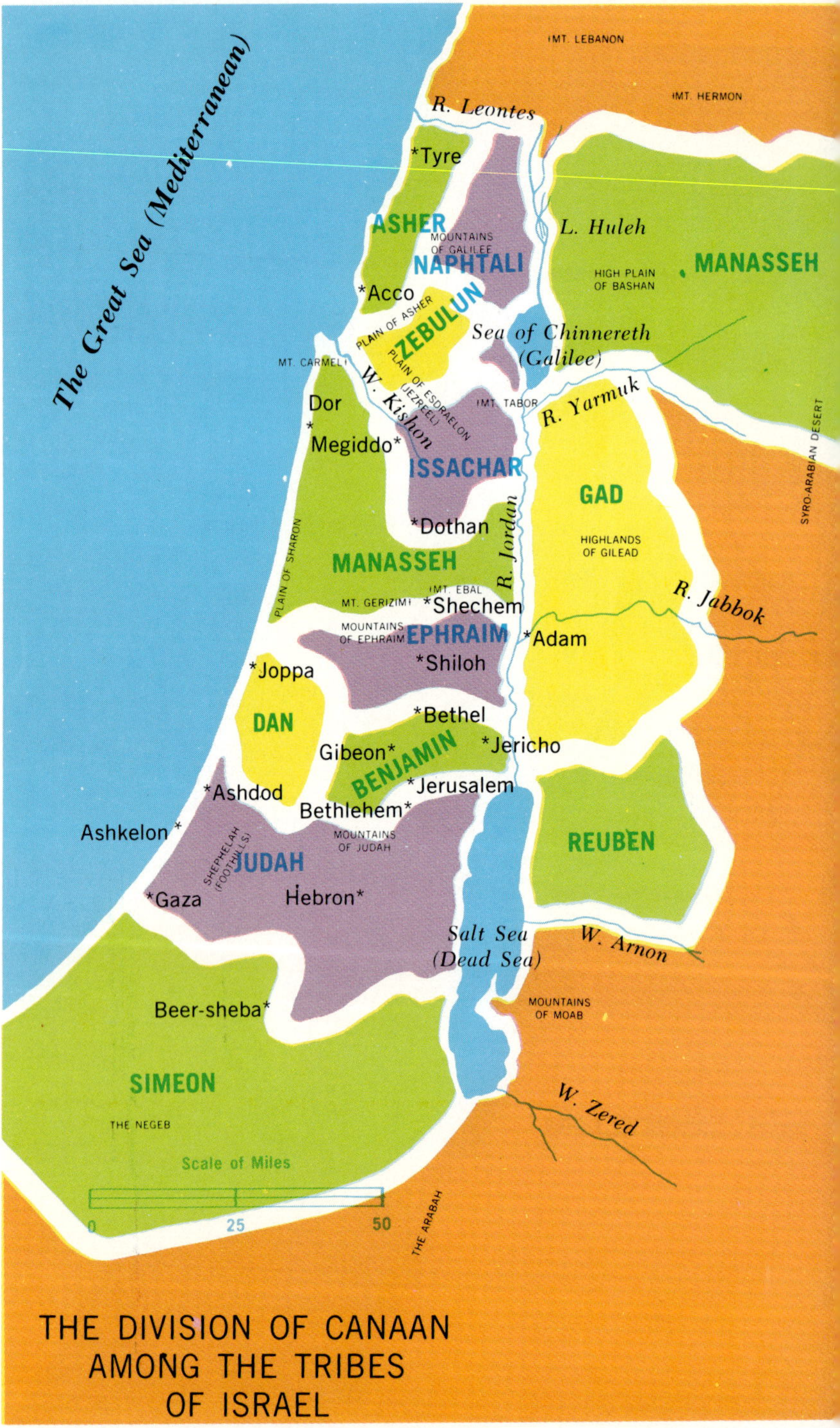

THE DIVISION OF CANAAN AMONG THE TRIBES OF ISRAEL

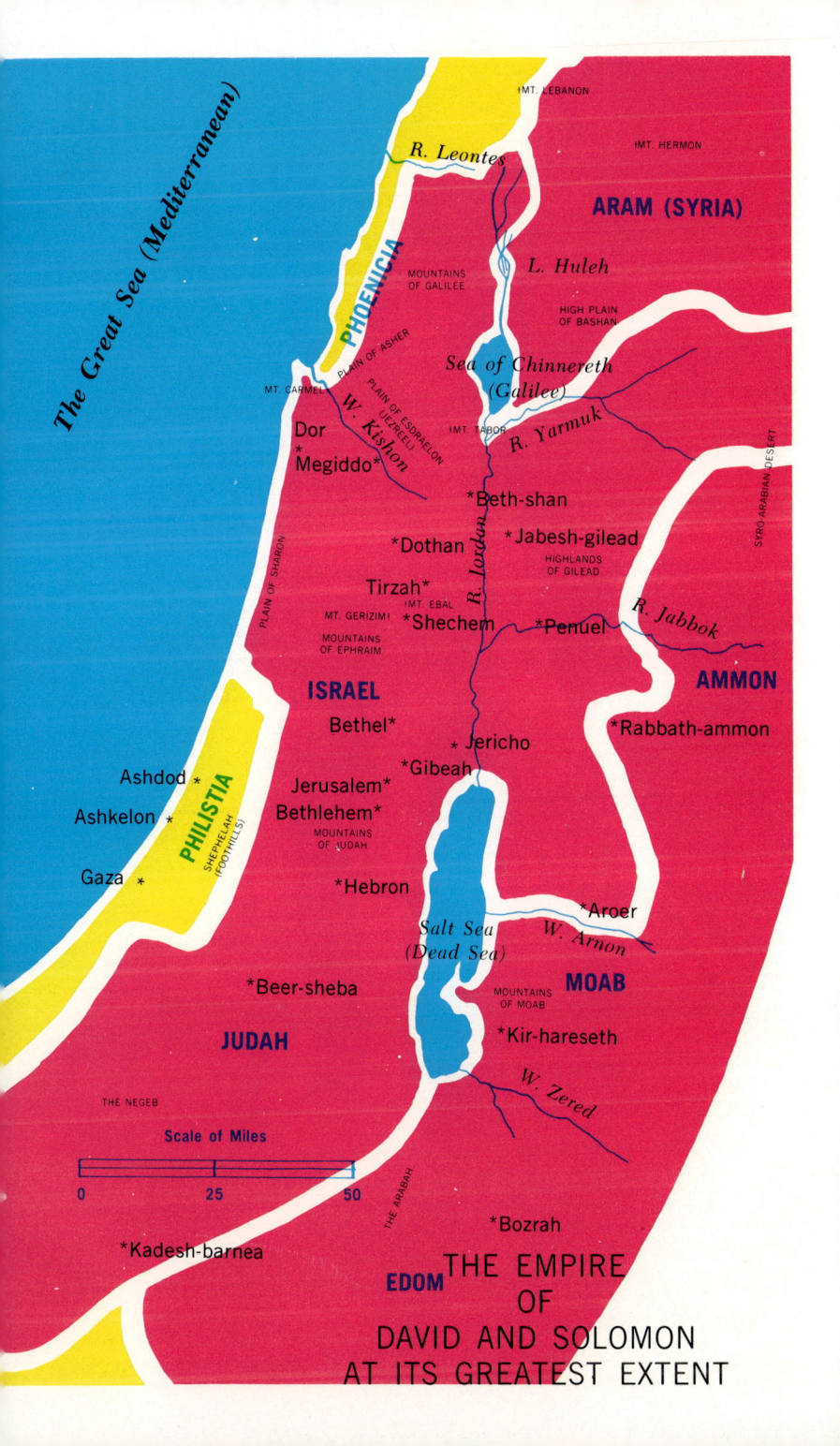

THE EMPIRE OF DAVID AND SOLOMON AT ITS GREATEST EXTENT

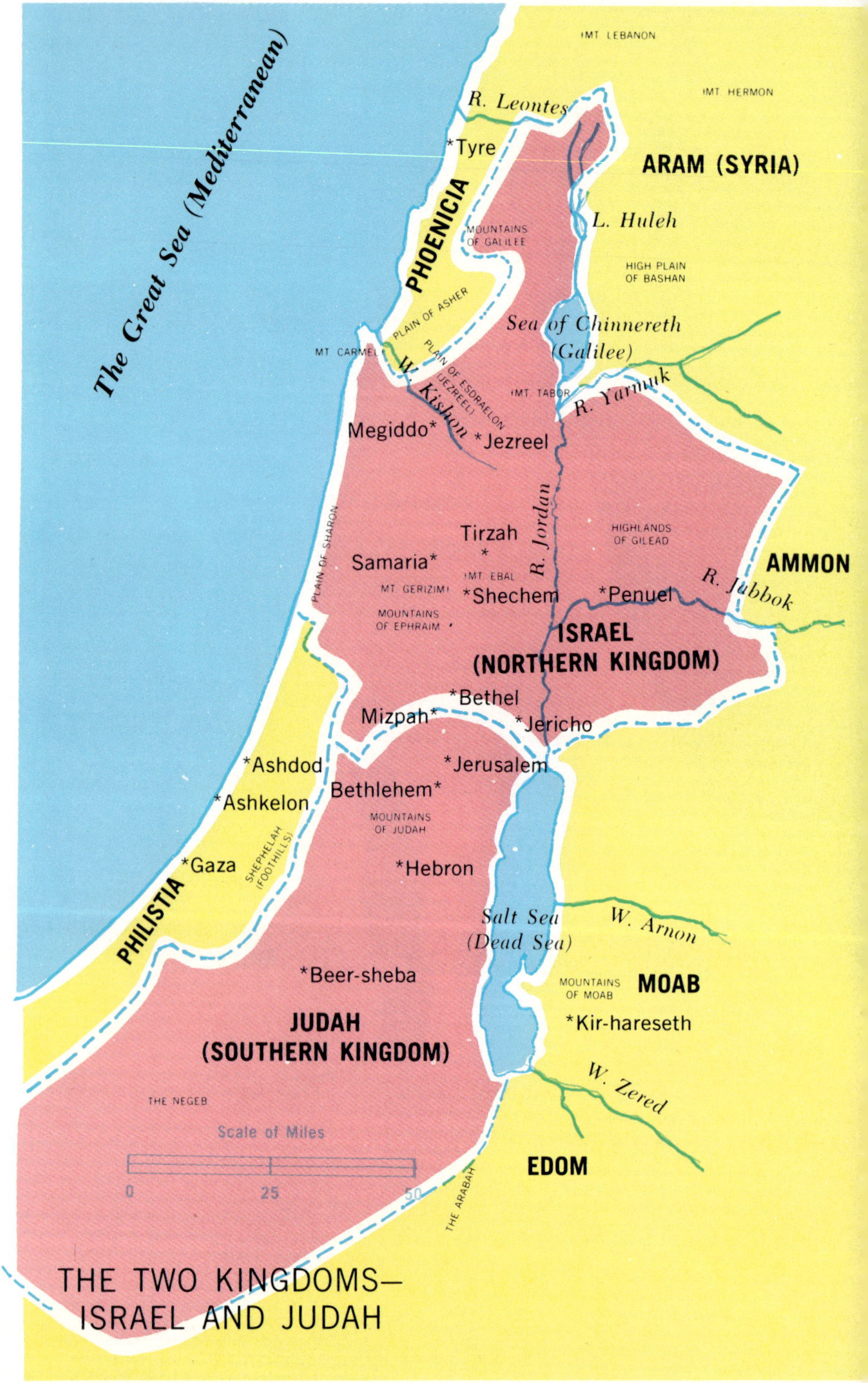

The Great Sea (Mediterranean)
MT. LEBANON
MT. HERMON
R. Leontes
*Tyre
ARAM (SYRIA)
PHOENICIA
MOUNTAINS OF GALILEE
L. Huleh
HIGH PLAIN OF BASHAN
PLAIN OF ASHER
Sea of Chinnereth (Galilee)
MT. CARMEL
W. Kishon
PLAIN OF ESDRAELON (JEZREEL)
MT. TABOR
R. Yarmuk
Megiddo*
*Jezreel
R. Jordan
PLAIN OF SHARON
Tirzah
HIGHLANDS OF GILEAD
AMMON
Samaria*
MT. EBAL
MT. GERIZIM
*Shechem
*Penuel
R. Jabbok
MOUNTAINS OF EPHRAIM
ISRAEL
(NORTHERN KINGDOM)
*Bethel
Mizpah*
*Jericho
*Ashdod
*Jerusalem
*Ashkelon
Bethlehem*
MOUNTAINS OF JUDAH
*Gaza
SHEPHELAH (FOOTHILLS)
*Hebron
PHILISTIA
Salt Sea (Dead Sea)
W. Arnon
*Beer-sheba
MOUNTAINS OF MOAB
MOAB
*Kir-hareseth
JUDAH
(SOUTHERN KINGDOM)
W. Zered
THE NEGEB
Scale of Miles
0
25
50
EDOM
THE ARABAH
THE TWO KINGDOMS—
ISRAEL AND JUDAH

JUDAH AFTER THE FALL OF ISRAEL

JUDAH AS A PERSIAN PROVINCE

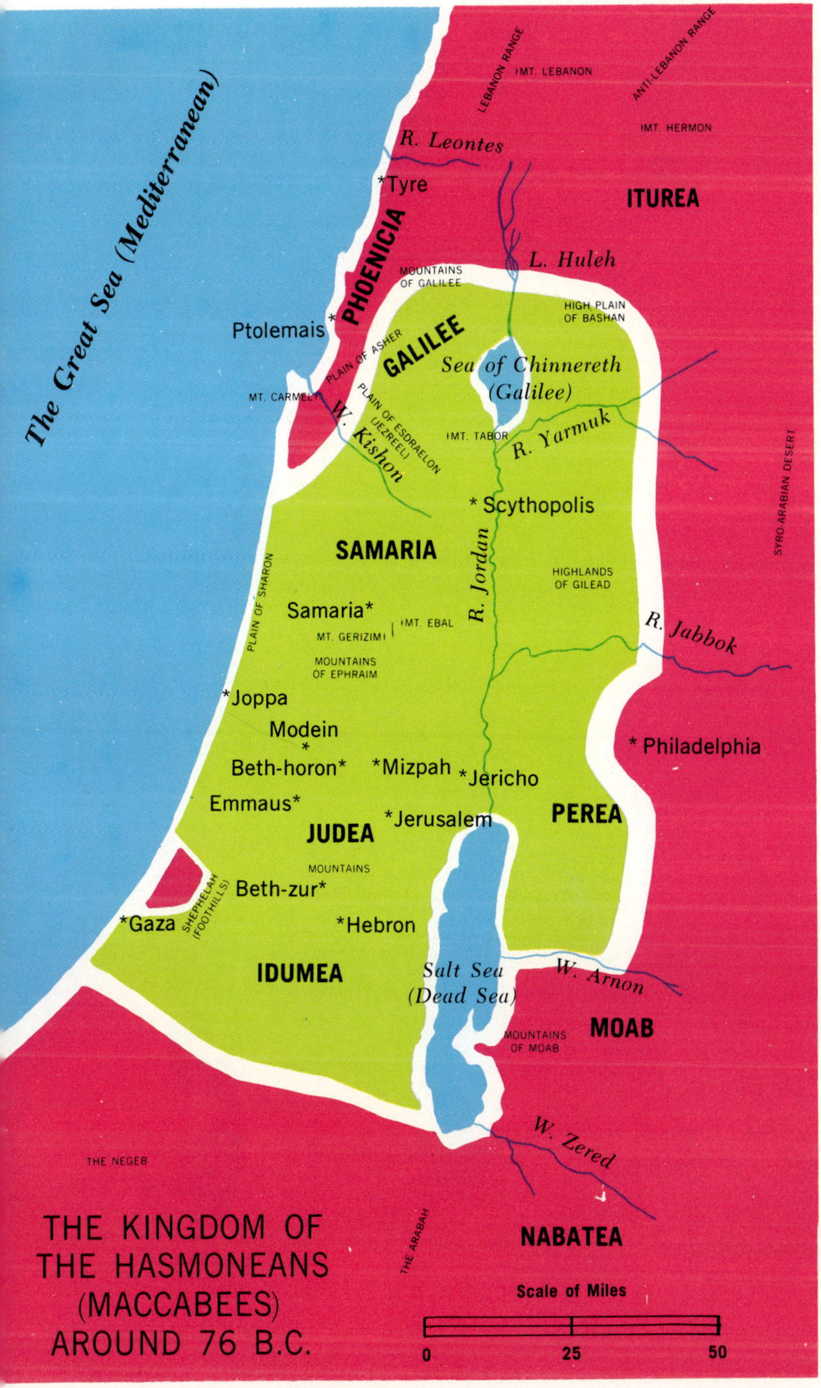

THE KINGDOM OF THE HASMONEANS (MACCABEES) AROUND 76 B.C.

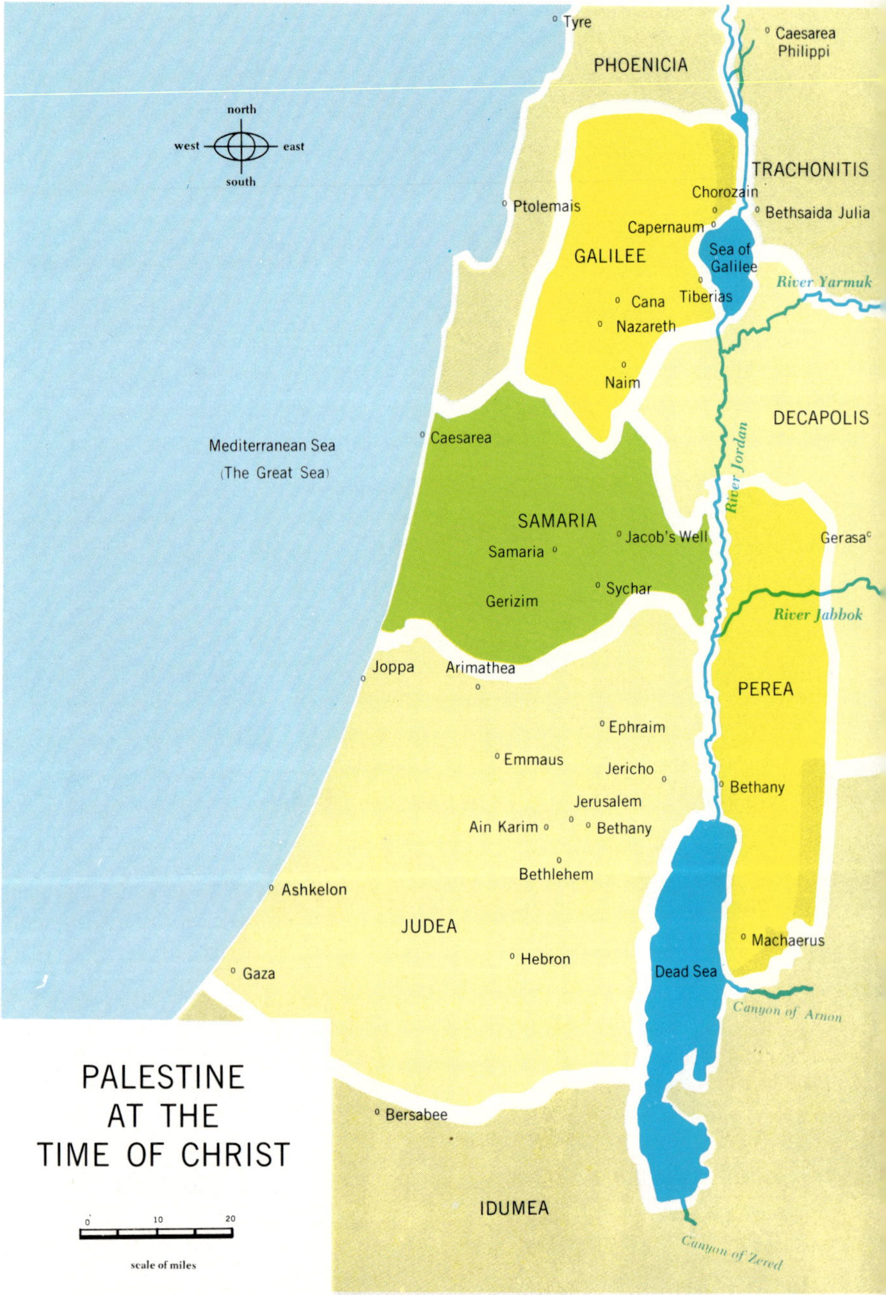

PALESTINE AT THE TIME OF CHRIST

THE CITY OF JERUSALEM

VALLEY
LOWER HILLSIDE
UPPER HILLSIDE
HIGHEST GROUND

- Pool of Bethesda
- Sheep Gate
- Roman Fortress of Antonia
- Gethsemane
- Holy Sepulchre
- Calvary
- THE TEMPLE
- Mt. Moriah
- Sanhedrin
- Palace of Maccabean Dynasty (Hasmoneans)
- Kidron Valley
- Praetorium of Pilate?
- Gardens
- UPPER CITY
- Home of Caiaphas
- Mt. Zion
- LOWER CITY
- Cenacle
- Pool of Siloam
- Ge-hinnom

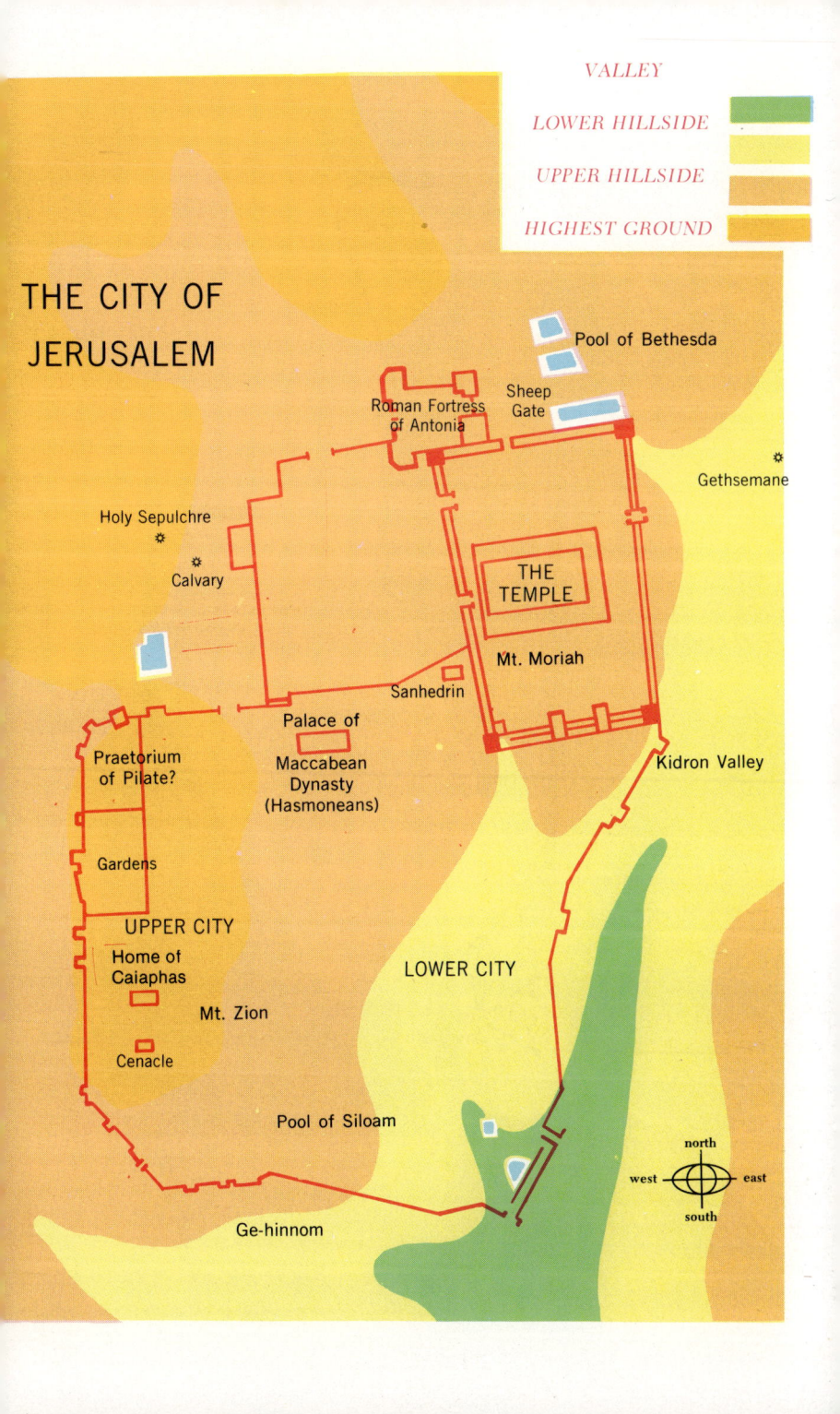

north / west / east / south

THE SPREAD OF THE GOSPEL BEGINS

blue-green arrows — journeys of Peter
black arrows — journeys of Philip
grey arrows — journeys of Barnabas
red arrows — journeys of Saul

ST PAUL'S FIRST MISSIONARY JOURNEY

ST. PAUL'S SECOND MISSIONARY JOURNEY

ST. PAUL'S THIRD MISSIONARY JOURNEY

ST. PAUL'S FOURTH MISSIONARY JOURNEY

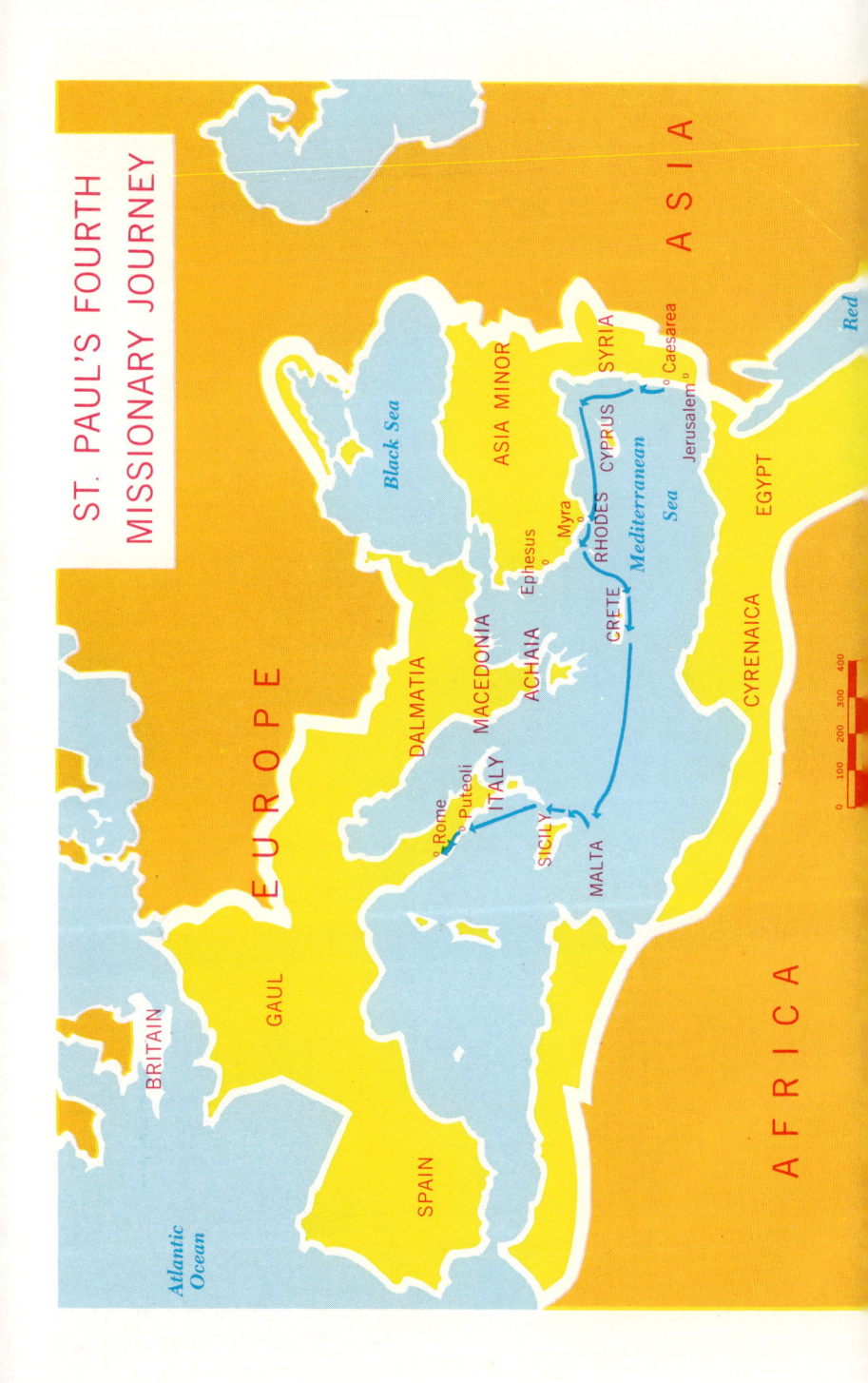

Left: ancient altar

Right: stele at Petra

ancient tower-temple

Egyptian boat and

land transport

construction work

musicians

Desert of Judah

Palestinian well today

desert transportation

fishing—Sea of Galilee

Qumran: the Dead Sea

Qumran: ruins

caves at Qumran

interior of cave

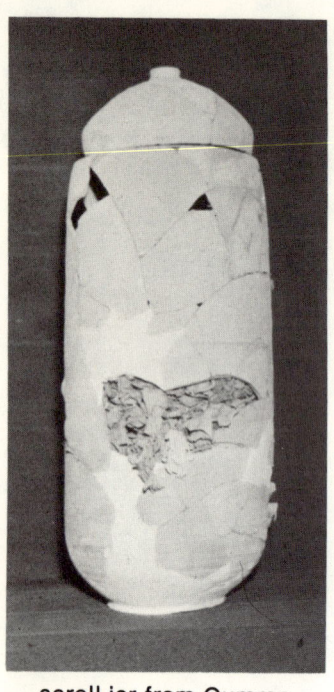

scroll-jar from Qumran

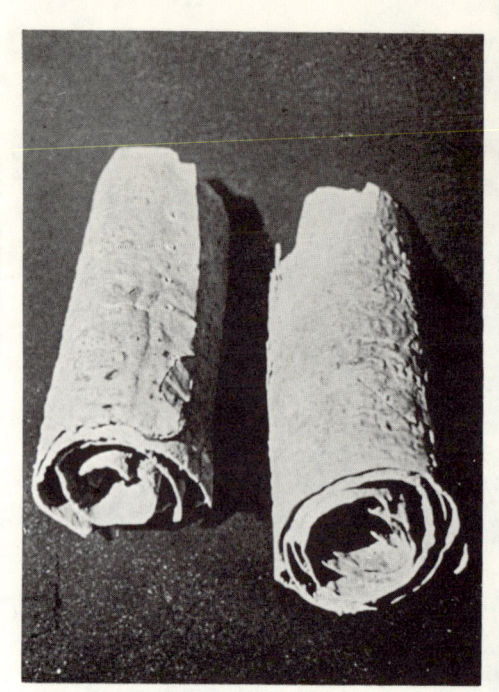

Qumran scrolls

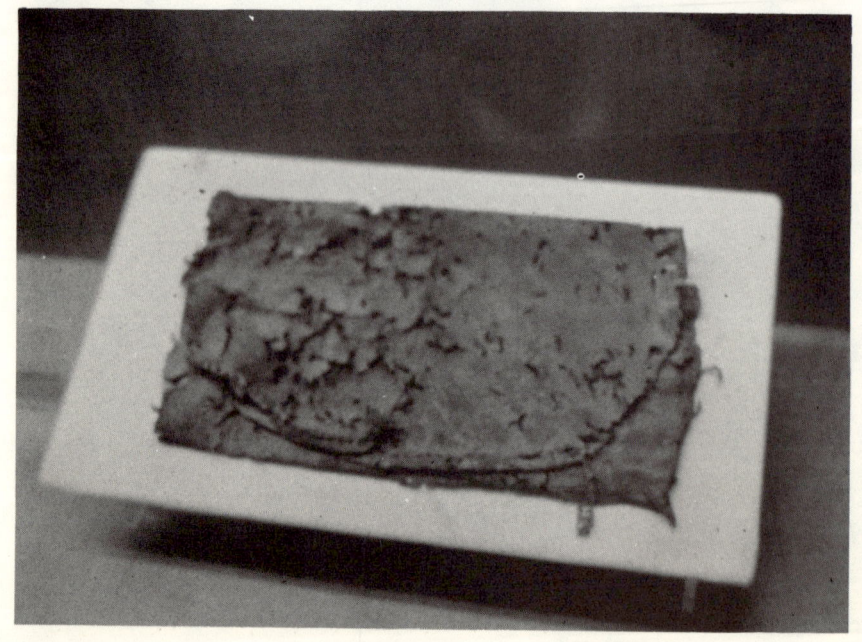

leather pouch, Qumran

scroll of Isaiah, Qumran

community scroll, Qumran

ENTADEKITEMAPIAΓY
NHCAΛOYTIOYOCTIC
KAΛWCEZHCENME
TATOYANΔPOCAYTHC
ENIPHNHHKOIMHCICAYHC

Hebrew inscription

biblical manuscript, fourth century: *Codex Vaticanus*

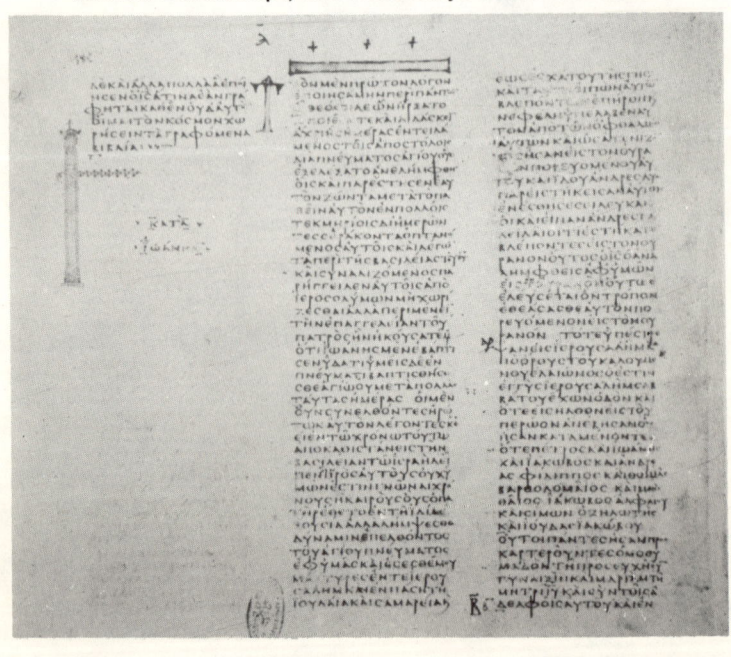

biblical manuscript, fourth century: *Codex Sinaiticus*

biblical fragment, second century: *Bodmer Papyrus*

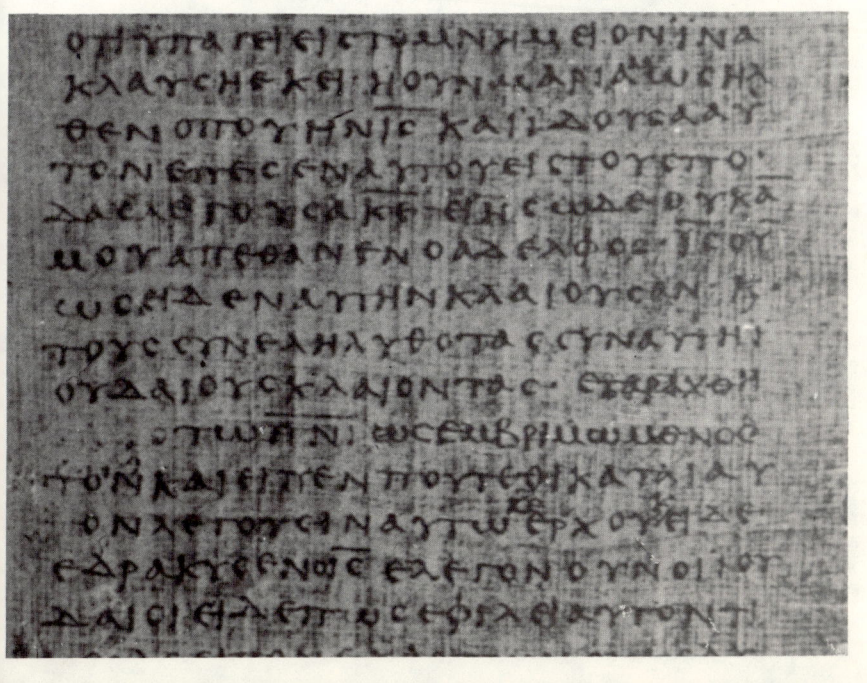

Nazareth, Church of the Annunciation

Nazareth, Grotto of the Annunciation

Bethlehem, Grotto of the Nativity   Jacob's Well, Samaria

Church of the Beatitudes, Galilee

Left: Tabgah, possible site of the multiplication of the loaves;
Right: Pool of Siloam, Jerusalem
Below: Herod's Temple (model)

Left: Wailing Wall, Temple of Jerusalem; *Right:* Cenacle, traditional site of the Last Supper
Below: Gethsemane, "Church of the Nations"

Pretorium of Pilate

Left: Basilica of the Holy Sepulcher; *Right:* Church of the Ascension

The New Testament

From the Dogmatic Constitution on Divine Revelation, ch. 5

The Word of God, which is the power of God for the salvation of all who believe (cf. Rom. 1:16), is set forth and shows its power in a most excellent way in the writings of the New Testament. For when the fullness of time arrived (cf. Gal. 4:4), the Word was made flesh and dwelt among us in His fullness of graces and truth (cf. Jn. 1:14). Christ established the kingdom of God on earth, manifested His Father and Himself by deeds and words, and completed His work by His death, resurrection and glorious ascension and by the sending of the Holy Spirit. Having been lifted up from the earth, He draws all men to Himself (cf. Jn. 12:32, Greek text), He who alone has the words of eternal life (cf. Jn. 6:68). This mystery had not been manifested to other generations as it was now revealed to His holy Apostles and prophets in the Holy Spirit (cf. Eph. 3:4-6, Greek text), so that they might preach the Gospel, stir up faith in Jesus, Christ and Lord, and gather together the Church. Now the writings of the New Testament stand as a perpetual and divine witness to these realities.

It is common knowledge that among all the Scriptures, even those of the New Testament, the Gospels have a special preeminence, and rightly so, for they are the principal witness for the life and teaching of the Incarnate Word, our Savior.

The Church has always and everywhere held and continues to hold that the four Gospels are of apostolic origin. For what the Apostles preached in fulfillment of the commission of Christ, afterwards they themselves and apostolic men, under the inspiration of the divine Spirit, handed on to us in writing: the foundation of faith, namely, the fourfold Gospel, according to Matthew, Mark, Luke and John.[1]

Holy Mother Church has firmly and with absolute constancy held, and continues to hold, that the four Gospels just named, whose historical character the

Church unhesitatingly asserts, faithfully hand on what Jesus Christ, while living among men, really did and taught for their eternal salvation until the day He was taken up into heaven (cf. Acts 1:1). Indeed, after the ascension of the Lord the Apostles handed on to their hearers what He had said and done. This they did with that clearer understanding which they enjoyed[2] after they had been instructed by the glorious events of Christ's life and taught by the light of the Spirit of truth.[3] The sacred authors wrote the four Gospels, selecting some things from the many which had been handed on by word of mouth or in writing, reducing some of them to a synthesis, explaining some things in view of the situation of their churches, and preserving the form of proclamation but always in such fashion that they told us the honest truth about Jesus.[4] For their intention in writing was that either from their own memory and recollections, or from the witness of those who "themselves from the beginning were eyewitnesses and ministers of the Word" we might know "the truth" concerning those matters about which we have been instructed (cf. Lk. 1:2-4).

Besides the four Gospels, the canon of the New Testament also contains the epistles of St. Paul and other apostolic writings, composed under the inspiration of the Holy Spirit, by which, according to the wise plan of God, those matters which concern Christ the Lord are confirmed, His true teaching is more and more fully stated, the saving power of the divine work of Christ is preached, the story is told of the beginnings of the Church and its marvelous growth, and its glorious fulfillment is foretold.

For the Lord Jesus was with His Apostles as He had promised (cf. Mt. 28:20) and sent them the advocate Spirit who would lead them into the fullness of truth (cf. Jn. 16:13).

---

1. Cf. St. Irenaeus, *Against Heretics* III, 11; 8:PG 7, 885, Sagnard Edition, p. 194. 2. John 2:22; 12:16; cf. 14:26; 16:12-13; 7:39. 3. Cf. John 14:26; 16:13. 4. Cf. Instruction *Holy Mother Church: AAS* 56 (1964) p. 715.

The Gospel According to St. Matthew

The Gospel ascribed to Matthew dates from after the destruction of Jerusalem in 70 A.D. Some think that a possible shorter Aramaic Gospel preceded the Greek one we have today. The latter, however, does not seem to be a translation of the former, but an adaptation of a new work. It was written for the believers who came from Judaism and shows that Jesus is really the Messiah foretold in the Scriptures, that He is God and that He founded a Church which is the kingdom of God on earth.

Jesus is the expectation of Israel, the fulfillment of God's promise. Matthew proves this with many citations from the Old Testament. Thirty-seven quotations are introduced with expressions such as: "This happened to fulfill what the Lord had spoken by the prophet...." Matthew thus underlines the fulfillment of the Old Testament prophecies in Jesus, "Son of David" and "Son of Abraham" (1:1): in the Virgin birth (1:23) at Bethlehem (2:5), in the flight into Egypt (2:15), the massacre of the Innocents (2:15), Jesus' life in Nazareth (2:23), His ministry in Galilee (4:14), His stay at Capernaum (4:14-16), Jesus' healing ministry (8:17), His teaching in parables (13:14), the entry into Jerusalem (21:4), the disciples desertion (26:31), the thirty pieces of silver (27:9), the arrest (26:54) and the three days burial (12:40).

Matthew's Gospel has been called the Gospel of the Kingdom, or the Gospel of the Church. In fact, Matthew speaks of the kingdom 51 times.

Christ came to establish this kingdom promised by the prophets. This kingdom on earth is the Church with Peter as its head. Jesus entrusted Peter with the power of the keys and made him the foundation of the Church: "...You are 'Rock,' and on this rock I will build my church.... I will entrust to you the keys of the kingdom of heaven" (16:18-19). Here the keys symbolize Peter's authority as leader of the Church of Christ. Peter, therefore, will exercise spiritual power over the new People of God.

The whole Gospel centers around the theme of the kingdom and can be divided into seven sections. There are five main discourses of Jesus which contain His teachings.

The Prologue (chapters 1 and 2) narrates the preparation for the kingdom in the child Messiah.

Chapters 3 through 7 contain the formal proclamation of the kingdom in which Jesus calls His first disciples (4:18) and begins to preach throughout Galilee (14:23). This section contains the first discourse (chapters 5-7), the Sermon on the Mount.

Jesus officially proclaims the Kingdom and its standards. Matthew presents Jesus as a second and greater Moses, a Lawgiver who repeats the Law but corrects it and raises it to heights undreamed of in the Old Testament (5:21-48).

He outlines the whole program of Christian life which is summed up in the beatitudes (5:3-12). The life and actions of every Christian must be measured against them.

Jesus makes greater demands on people than did the Law of Moses, but He bestows the grace needed for meeting these demands (Rom. 8:1-11). His disciples are bound to respond to the divine gift (5:20). Though the Sermon on the Mount is concerned with the relationship between God and the individual, its social implications are evident.

Chapters 8-10 relate the preaching of the kingdom, a preaching confirmed by miracles (8:1, 5, 14, 16; 9:1, 18, 27, 32).

The second discourse is the apostolic discourse, or the mission instructions (chapter 10). In this discourse Jesus begins to form the nucleus of His Kingdom, the apostolic Church. He chooses the Apostles and sends them to preach the Word. He tells them that they must be ready for persecution (10:17-25) and thus resemble their Teacher. He exhorts them to a fearless confession of faith (10:26-33). He spells out the conditions of discipleship.

Chapters 11 through 13 of Matthew's Gospel show that the Kingdom of God does not accord with human expectations (11:16-25). Therefore Jesus meets opposition (12:2, 10-15, 24, 38).

The third discourse is made up of the parables of the Kingdom (chapter 13). With them Jesus revealed the mystery of the Kingdom.

Chapters 14 through 18 narrate the early development of the Kingdom in the Church, i.e., the group of disciples with Peter at their head (16:13-20).

The fourth discourse treats rules governing the new community. The apostolic Church was a true society. In this discourse, Jesus teaches the members of the new People of God the relations that should exist among them: humility, good example, prayer, love and forgiveness (chapter 18).

The increasing hostility of the Jewish leaders occasions the crisis found in chapters 19 through 25. Jesus condemns the hypocrisy of the Scribes and Pharisees (19:3; 21:15-16, 23, 46; 22:15, 34-35).

The fifth discourse is eschatological, announcing the consummation of the Kingdom (chapters 24-25). In it Jesus says that it will be the task of the disciples to announce the Gospel of the Kingdom to all the nations (24:14). He also teaches that the Christian community is to be ever ready to meet the Lord at His second coming; to function with a sense of personal responsibility for divine gifts received, and to be constantly aware of the primacy of love of neighbor (25:31-46).

Chapters 26-28 make up the seventh section and relate the establishment of the Kingdom through Christ's passion, death and resurrection. Chapter 28 records Jesus' resurrection, the apparitions of the risen

Lord and the mission given to His disciples, which embraces the whole world.

The last words of the Master: "Know that I am with you always, until the end of the world!" will ever sustain those whom the risen Lord has commissioned to preach the "Good News" of salvation.

The Gospel of St. Matthew was the most widely diffused in the Church from the very beginning, because it presents a synthesis of the testimony of the Apostles concerning the teaching and the life of Jesus; His messianity and divinity; His Kingdom and the redemptive work fulfilled by Him, our Savior, for the salvation of mankind.

STUDY QUESTIONS

1. *When was the Gospel of St. Matthew written, and who was it written for?*
2. *What does this Gospel show us?*
3. *What has Matthew's Gospel been called and why?*
4. *How is this Kingdom described in Matthew's Gospel?*
5. *How is Matthew's Gospel divided?*
6. *In what does the first discourse consist?*
7. *In what does the second discourse consist?*
8. *In what does the third discourse consist?*
9. *In what does the fourth discourse consist?*
10. *In what does the fifth discourse consist?*
11. *Why was the Gospel of St. Matthew the most widely diffused in the Church from the very beginning?*

The Gospel According to St. Mark

Who exactly was Mark? He is also surnamed John Mark, not one of the Twelve. But he takes part with his cousin Barnabas in the first missions of Paul (Acts 12:25ff.). Then he separates himself from Paul (Acts 13:13). But we find him again later when Paul is in prison (Col. 4:10; Phlm. 24). Papias of Hierapolis, writing about 110 A.D., speaks about "Mark, the interpreter of Peter, who wrote accurately, but not in order, all that he recalled of the words or actions of the Lord." It is Mark who gives us the earliest, shortest and simplest Gospel, written to show the Romans that Jesus is the Son of God.

From the beginning, in fact, Mark brings his reader into vital contact with the mystery of Christ. One is invited to fix his mind's gaze on Christ, God Incarnate, his personal Savior and Redeemer. In fact, his opening words are, "Here begins the gospel of Jesus Christ, the Son of God" (1:1).

The Gospel of St. Mark answers two fundamental questions: Who is this Man? "The Messiah" (1:14—8:30) and, What kind of Messiah? "The mystery of the Son of Man" (8:31—16:20).

Jesus is the Revelation of the Father, the way to the Father. Men are asked to "reform and believe" (1:15) and be saved. "...The man who refuses to believe in it will be condemned" (16:16).

A feature of the Gospel of Mark, in particular, is what is called the "messianic secret," the apparent unwillingness of Jesus to become publicly known as "Messiah." This attitude of Jesus may seem strange to us at first, since Jesus was the Messiah, and had come to make Himself known to the world as such. But it becomes understandable when we realize that the kind of messiah the crowds were looking for was a purely earthly messiah, a powerful political leader (like Judas Maccabeus) who would drive away the Roman conquerer and so free His people. Because of this, Jesus could not openly declare Himself without compromising His spiritual mission. Hence the frequent use by Him of the title "Son of Man" (2:10, 28; 8:38; 9:31; 10:33; 14:41) to designate Himself. This title, as used in Daniel 7:13, had a messianic reference. But the crowds were less familiar with it and did not understand it as messianic. It should be noted that when Jesus was on trial and officially questioned by the Sanhedrin, "Are you the Messiah, the Son of the Blessed One?" (14:61), He unhesitatingly answered, "I am." In so doing, He knew this would be interpreted as blasphemy, which carried the penalty of death.

Mark wrote his Gospel around 70 A.D., in Rome, in the Greek language, which was then known and spoken even in Rome. According to ancient testimonies, the Christians themselves, eager to conserve Peter's preaching, asked Mark to put it into writing.

Since it was addressed to non-Jews, Mark explains Jewish customs (7:3-5, 12:18, 14:36, 15:34) and translates Aramaic words used by Jesus (5:41; 7:11, 34). Mark's style is clear and colorful, and he knows how to make a scene come alive by the use of details. For example, Jesus looked "with love" (10:21) or "with anger" (3:5). He points out Jesus' tenderness (9:36; 10:16, 21), His irritation (1:43), 8:12, 10:14) and other details not mentioned by the other Evangelists (3:34, 5:32, 10:23, 11:11). He even notes Jesus had slept on a cushion in the boat during the storm on the lake (4:38).

Completely omitting accounts of the infancy of Jesus, Mark has a brief introduction (1:1-13) and then immediately proceeds to Jesus' ministry in Galilee (1:14—7:23) and outside of Galilee (7:24—8:30). From chapters 8:31 through 10:52, he narrates the journey to Jerusalem, and in chapters 11 through 13, the ministry in Jerusalem. The Gospel concludes with a detailed narration of the passion, death and resurrection of the Savior (chapters 14-16).

Mark repeatedly underscores the fact that the passion and death of Jesus did not happen by chance, but was an essential part of the mysterious plan of God for the salvation of mankind (cf. also Acts 4:28).

Writing for Christian converts from paganism, Mark not only aims at giving the apostolic preaching in its substantial integrity, but he especially wishes to clearly show the divinity of Jesus Christ.

The Father Himself testifies that Jesus is God (1:11, 9:7), as do the demons (1:24, 3:11, 5:7) and men (15:39). Jesus claims the power to forgive sin (2:10), which belongs to God alone, and proves that He is God by miracles (1:40-45; 6:30-44, 45-52; 7:31-37, 24-30, etc.) and by exorcisms (3:7-12, 23; 9:14-29).

Mark abundantly recounts those miracles of Jesus that are more suited to attracting attention and sustaining faith. He does not say much that is new, but he has the privilege of vividly handing on the testimony of him who was chosen by Jesus to be His own representative on earth—Peter!

The reading of Mark's Gospel helps us to fix our gaze on Christ, God Incarnate, and to ask for a faith like that which must have shone out in Peter's preaching.

STUDY QUESTIONS

1. *When and where was the Gospel of St. Mark written and why was it written?*
2. *Who was St. Mark?*
3. *Why did Mark write his Gospel?*
4. *What is the message that Mark brings out in his Gospel?*
5. *What is a feature of the Gospel of Mark?*
6. *How is Mark's Gospel divided?*
7. *What was Mark's aim in writing to the Christian converts from paganism?*

The Gospel According to St. Luke

Luke wrote his Gospel before the Acts, perhaps around the year 70 A.D. He gathered his material from an existing written collection about Jesus and also received information from Jesus' disciples and Jesus' mother.

A pagan by birth and a physician by profession, Luke became, after his conversion, a disciple and a missionary companion of St. Paul. He accompanied and assisted the Apostle of the Gentiles until Paul's death. With him he shared the concepts of the universality of salvation and the mercy of God for all men. Thus, both of these ideas are clearly reflected in his Gospel, which he wrote for the Gentiles, especially for all those who—like Theophilus, God's friend—desire to know and live Jesus' message. Luke's purpose is to show that Jesus is the Lord and Savior of all mankind.

Luke's Gospel opens with the description of the Annunciation, birth and infancy of Jesus (chapters 1-2). This infancy narrative is the most detailed of all the Gospels. The author follows Mark's general plan. The introduction to the ministry (3:1—4:13) is followed by Jesus' ministry in Galilee (4:14—9:50), the journey to Jerusalem (9:51—19:27) and His ministry there (19:28—21:38). He concludes with the passion, death and burial (chapters 22-23) and Jesus's resurrection and ascension (chapter 24).

Luke presents much more than Mark. All the events placed between 9:51 and 18:14 in Luke are not found in Mark.

Seemingly a man of meek, peaceful character and marked sensibility, Luke stresses the goodness of the Lord and Jesus' love for sinners (15:1-2, 7, 10). In Jesus, sinners find a "friend" (7:34) who associates with them (15:1-2). Jesus pardons the penitent woman (7:36-50), the rich publican, Zaccheus (19:1-10), and His very executioners (23:34). He goes after the lost sheep (15:4-7) and assures that the return of the repentant sinner enjoys the special favor of God (15:1-32).

Luke also emphasizes our Savior's concern for the poor: the Good News is preached to the poor (7:22; 4:18); the poor are called blessed and enter the kingdom of heaven (6:20).

Another special characteristic of Luke is his insistence on prayer. Jesus loves to draw apart by Himself to pray (6:12) and is often found in prayer, for example, at His baptism (3:21), before the choice of the Apostles (6:12), at the Transfiguration (9:28) and when He is crucified (23:34). He also teaches us how to pray (11:1-13; 18:1-14, etc.) and how to be confident and persevering in prayer (11:9-13). Actual prayers, too, are recorded in Luke's Gospel: the Our Father (11:24), the *Benedictus* (2:68-79), the *Magnificat* (2:46-55), the *Gloria in Excelsis* (3:14).

In Luke we meet Mary, the Mother of Jesus. We see her at the Annunciation (1:26ff.), at the visitation (1:39ff.), at Jesus' birth (2:4ff.), at the presentation in the Temple (2:22ff.), during her Son's infancy, childhood (2:42ff.), and public life. Luke speaks of her personal sanctity (1:28) and her divine mission (1:31).

Luke also manifests Jesus' gentle attitude toward women, who were so despised at His time. He shows consideration and respect for them (7:36-49, 8:43-48).

Even foreigners are the object of Jesus's care. For example, He cures the son of the centurion (7:1-10) and rebukes His disciples when they suggest that fire be called down from heaven to destroy the unfriendly Samaritans (9:54-56).

Luke insists on the necessity of self-denial for becoming a disciple of Jesus (18:29), and on complete renunciation as a condition required for following the Master (12:33; 14:26, 33). He explains the demands made by the Gospel message: One must take up his cross *daily* (9:23).

Above all, Luke gives a clear presentation of the Holy Spirit and how He fills the hearts of believers with peace and joy. The Holy Spirit permeates the Gospel of Luke: We meet Him in the infancy narratives (1:35, 41, 67; 2:25-27) and often during Jesus' public life (4:1, 14, 18; 10:21). The Lord's disciples, too, are promised that they will be helped by the Holy Spirit in time of persecution (12:12).

The Gospel of Luke has been called the Gospel of Joy—joy to the world—not only because first and foremost it announces salvation *to all mankind* (24:47), but also because the evangelist breathes throughout an atmosphere of joy, gladness, peace, thanksgiving and glorification of God.

STUDY QUESTIONS

1. *When did Luke write his Gospel and who did he write it for?*
2. *Who was St. Luke?*
3. *What sources did Luke use for his Gospel?*
4. *What concepts did St. Luke share with St. Paul?*
5. *What is the purpose of Luke's Gospel?*
6. *What characteristics of Jesus does Luke stress?*
7. *What other person does Luke bring out in his Gospel?*
8. *What spirit is needed for becoming a disciple of Jesus according to Luke's Gospel?*
9. *How does St. Luke describe the Holy Spirit in his Gospel?*
10. *Why is the Gospel of St. Luke called the Gospel of Joy?*

The Gospel According to St. John

John presents the Person and work of the Lord in a way that is different from the other evangelists. As they did, John is also writing history. His Gospel is very accurate in this respect. His references to the geography of Palestine, for example, are amazingly exact. But John goes beyond the mere facts to a theological reflection upon them.

He explains the meaning of the events, and seeks to lead the reader to faith in Jesus. John's profound insight into the mystery of the Incarnate Word is why his Gospel is often called a spiritual Gospel.

Written some time between 90-100 A.D., John's was the last Gospel to be written. It has behind it not only the apostolic preaching and synoptic tradition, but the reflection and prayer of a whole generation of Christians.

The Person of Jesus, the Revealer of the Father, is the central theme of the Gospel. John focuses on the Incarnation and its meaning for us. The opening words of John's First Epistle express this:

"This is what we proclaim to you:
what was from the beginning,
what we have heard,
what we have seen with our eyes,
what we have looked upon
and our hands have touched—
we speak of the word of life.
(...that was present to the Father
and became visible to us.)
...we proclaim in turn to you
so that you may share life with us.

This fellowship of ours is with the Father
and with his Son, Jesus Christ" (1 Jn. 1:1, 2, 3).

John's special concern is with the divinity of Christ. He selects certain miracles or signs of Jesus, and presents them to the reader. He shows the meaning of these signs as they point to Jesus' divine power. Jesus reveals Himself only gradually. But this gradual revelation is accompanied by a growing hostility from those who will not accept Jesus. The theme of light and darkness, a favorite one for John, expresses this clash. Light is associated with God. Jesus is the Light of the world, and those who follow Him walk in His light.

St. John's Gospel is outlined thus:

1. *The Prologue* (1:1-18)
   A summary of the Gospel message:
   "The Word became flesh
   ...and we have seen his glory:
   ...filled with enduring love" (1:14).
2. *The Book of Signs* (1:19—12:50)
   The Word Incarnate reveals Himself to the world through words (6:35; 8:12, 58; 10:9, 11; 11:25; 14:6; 15:1) *and works* (2:1-11, 13-22; 4:46-54; 5:1-9; 6:1-15, 16-21; 9:1-7; 11:1-46).
3. *The Book of Glory* (chapters 13-21)
   The Word Incarnate reveals Himself in suffering and glory. The Jesus of John is a Jesus of glory even in the passion, and the cross is His "exaltation."

In the Gospel of John, *faith* is a fundamental theme. Its *object* is almost exclusively *the Person of Jesus*.

Jesus is the meeting place of two worlds, the human and the divine. In the risen Jesus, we encounter the Father through the Holy Spirit.

It seems that John wanted to deepen the faith of Christians, particularly the second-generation Christians (and Christians of all times).

Faith in the risen Christ was the source of the intrepid courage of the early Church.

Peace is another important theme in John (14:27; 16:33).

The first words of the risen Jesus to His disciples, as recorded by John, are: *"Peace* be with you." There is no mention of the failure of the disciples, no reproach of any kind, just "Peace."

These words of Jesus, "Peace be with you," combined with the giving of the Holy Spirit, were not mere words, but actually created peace in their hearts.

It is significant that the giving of the Holy Spirit is accompanied (in 20:23) by the conferring of the *power to forgive sins,* namely, to give to all mankind the fruits of Christ's sacrifice on the cross.

The Gospel of John is the Gospel for us of today, for it shows Christ as eternally present and acting in and through His Church and her sacraments, especially Baptism and the Eucharist. Through these, the redeeming grace of the historic events that took place in Palestine is extended to men down the centuries. John seems to say to us: You need not look back to the past. Live right now the life of the risen Jesus through His Spirit in the Church of the living God.

STUDY QUESTIONS

1. *How does St. John write history in his Gospel?*
2. *Why is the fourth Gospel called a spiritual Gospel?*
3. *On what is the Gospel of St. John centered?*
4. *What is the heart of John's Gospel message?*
5. *How is St. John's Gospel outlined?*
6. *What is the fundamental theme and object of John's Gospel?*
7. *What is another important theme of John's Gospel?*
8. *Why is the Gospel of John important for us today?*

The Acts of the Apostles

The Acts of the Apostles, generally regarded as the sequel to the Gospel of St. Luke, seems to have been written not later than the year 70 A.D. Luke's aim was to write the history of the beginnings of Christianity. Based on all the sources at the author's disposal and on his personal experience, the Acts of the Apostles gives us precious insights into the life of the primitive Church.

This book especially relates how the Gospel message was transmitted, as Jesus had mandated the Apostles, "You are to be my witnesses in Jerusalem, throughout Judea and Samaria, yes, even to the ends of the earth" (1:8, 9).

It centers around the activity of two key personalities: Sts. Peter and Paul. The first part (chapters 1-12) covers a span of twelve years. It revolves around Peter, the head of the Apostles, and tells of the Church's beginnings in Jerusalem, its growth in Judea and Samaria and its establishment at Antioch. The persecution which started with the martyrdom of Stephen caused the Christians to flee from Jerusalem. Wherever they went, they spread the Good News of Christ.

The second part (chapters 13-28) covers about twenty years. It narrates the progress of the Church among the pagans, especially in Antioch and Asia. It follows Saint Paul in his apostolic journeys through Asia Minor and Europe and ends with his imprisonment in Rome.

Although the Acts was written in narrative form, it is especially valuable for its theological viewpoint. In fact, the author shows the Church as a mystery of God and the bearer of the Word of salvation. The speeches (2:14-40; 3:12-26; 10:34-43; 13:16-41) recorded in this book also show the substance of the primitive Christian message, which is centered on the death and resurrection of Christ, the outpouring of the Holy Spirit and the new life in Christ through Baptism. Moreover, the Acts of the Apostles shows the close union between the Church and the Holy Spirit (2:1-4), from the time of the Spirit's descent on the Jerusalem community at Pentecost to initiate the Apostles into their mission, through the various stages of the Church's early expansion and growth (2:38; 8:15, 17; 10:19, 44-47; 11:15, 16, 24; 13:2; 15:8, 28; 16:6, 7; 20:22, 23, 28; 21:11; 28:25). The Spirit intervenes in each crisis, giving life, guidance and a missionary impulse. The Acts of the Apostles has also been called the "Gospel of the Holy Spirit."

The Acts complements and crowns the Gospel of St. Luke. This book is a compendium of the Gospel and it shows how the first Christians lived the Gospel. "They devoted themselves to the Apostles' instruction and the communal life, to the breaking of bread and the prayers" (2:42).

St. Luke gives special importance to prayer. Most of the important events are accompanied by prayer (1:14, 23; 2:2; 4:24-30; 6:6; 9:11; 10:2, 9ff.; 13:2f.).

Luke also stresses the unity of the early Christians. "The community of believers were of one heart and one mind" (Acts 4:32).

The reader of the Acts of the Apostles experiences a spiritual joy which is a fruit of the Holy Spirit, the same Holy Spirit who strengthens us to live as the Apostles and early Christians did—as witnesses of the risen Christ!

STUDY QUESTIONS

1. *When was the Acts of the Apostles written? What is the aim of the book and who wrote it?*
2. *What does the book especially relate?*
3. *Who are the two key personalities in the Acts of the Apostles?*

4. *Why is the Acts valuable, and what literary form was used in this book?*
5. *What is the substance of the speeches recorded in this book?*
6. *What else does the Acts show?*
7. *What important details does Luke give?*

The Letter of Paul to the Romans

Now we begin the reading of the Letters of St. Paul.

Paul, also called Saul (Acts 13:9), was a Jew with a Greek cultural background. Born in Tarsus of Cilicia (Acts 9:11, 21:39, 22:3) around 10 A.D., of parents from the tribe of Benjamin (Rom. 11:1, Phil. 3:5), Paul was also a Roman citizen (Acts 16:37f; 22:25-28; 23:27). He was educated in Jerusalem by Gamaliel (Acts 5:34), from whom he gained a thorough knowledge of the Mosaic Law and the prophets, becoming a "Pharisee...above reproaches when it came to justice based on the law" (Phil. 3:5, 6).

As a young man perhaps in his mid or late-twenties, Paul stood out for his hatred and persecution of the "new way" of nascent Christianity (Acts 22:4). After concurring in Stephen's martyrdom (Acts 7:58), Paul, "breathing murderous threats against the Lord's disciples" (Acts 9:1), fanatically persecuted the Church of Jesus, whom he did not know. But this Jesus waited for him on the road to Damascus and transformed the fiery devastator of the Christian flock into a zealous apostle.

One day, while Paul (then called Saul) was on his way toward Damascus, he was suddenly surrounded by a brilliant light, and fell to the ground. Then he heard a voice:

"Saul, Saul, why do you persecute me?"

"Who are you, Lord?"

"I am Jesus, whom you are persecuting," came the answer (cf. Acts 9:4-9). And Saul knew then that Jesus Christ was truly God; he immediately began to love Him ardently and energetically.

St. Paul was so sincere in his conversion that he wrote later: "I thank Christ Jesus our Lord, who has strengthened me, that he has made me his servant and judged me faithful. I was once a blasphemer, a persecutor, a man filled with arrogance.... The grace of our Lord has been granted me in overflowing measure.... To the King of ages, the immortal, the invisible, the only God, be honor and glory forever and ever! Amen" (1 Tm. 1:12-13, 14, 17).

The importance of the conversion of St. Paul is extraordinary for the history of the Church, and especially for us, children of the Gentiles, who have attained our redemption through his preaching.

The risen Lord revealed to Paul that He had chosen him to be the apostle of the pagans in the Greco-Roman world. Later, his mission as apostle to the Gentiles was formally approved by Peter and the pillars of the Church in Jerusalem (cf. Gal. 2:9).

In his world-wide mission, St. Paul imitated Jesus, the Divine Master. Paul called Jesus' Gospel, "my Gospel," and preached it passionately and selflessly for the rest of his life, because, as he wrote, "[The Gospel] is the power of God leading everyone who believes in it to salvation" (Rom. 1:16). Nothing stopped him from preaching the love of Christ—neither hard work nor exhaustion, neither dangers nor sufferings (1 Cor. 4:9-13). Instead, he rejoiced in all these because they helped him to be more like his crucified Lord (Rom. 8:35-39, 2 Cor. 4:10f.). He traveled thousands of miles for more than thirty years. St. Anselm said that Paul was never wanting to the people.

Besides founding and visiting many of the Churches of the Gentile world, Paul wrote them letters which are commentaries on certain points of doctrine that he had preached. These letters give us all the essentials of Paul's message.

It is important to remember that St. Paul does not presume to sum up his total teaching in any of his letters. The doctrine which he sets forth is always a part of the whole. He presents it in response to a particular need or situation. For example, Paul wrote to the Corinthians about the Holy Eucharist only because of the disorders which had crept in. He supposes the Christians to whom he writes, however, to be in possession of the totality of his message, which he had preached to them in sermons while he was among them. This does not detract from the value of the letters. They give us all the essentials of Paul's message.

His basic teaching was that Christ died to redeem us, and that He rose from the dead. He adapted this basic doctrine to his listeners. He developed it and enriched it, under the guidance of the Holy Spirit. He produced a body of literature without comparison. The power, stemming from his august simplicity, conquers hearts. His letters delighted Christians, enthused Chrysostom, converted Augustine and drew admiration even from pagans, who, according to St. John Chrysostom, used to argue as to who should have precedence—Paul or Plato.

Paul wrote his letters in Greek, in his own unique style, much more concerned with the message than with the form. In many cases, he creates Christian terminology by using words in an original way, or coining new ones to express the deepest truths. The novelty of his language and the profundity of his ideas rendered him obscure at times, even to his contemporaries (2 Pt. 3:16). He is a writer whose thoughts crowd around his pen, so to speak, and pour themselves into words and phrases packed with a great density of meaning. At first sight they seem to be quite difficult, but the best way to understand them is to love St. Paul and to read and reread them.

They are the most beautiful commentary on the Gospels, recognized immediately not as the words of man, but of God, "just as...the rest of Scripture" (2 Pt. 3:16).

Between the years 57 and 58 A.D., while Paul was in Corinth, he wrote the Letter to the Romans. Having already covered the territory in the eastern world, he was now looking for new fields to evangelize in the

West. Thus, he was considering a missionary journey to Spain, and planned to visit the Christians in Rome on his way there. He had been informed (perhaps by Aquila and Prisca [Acts 18:2]) that the Roman community was a mixed congregation of converted Jews and converted pagans—fervent, yes, but in danger of looking down on one another. The first Roman Christians had been among the Jews and proselytes who had heard Peter's Pentecost discourse in Jerusalem (Acts 2:10, 14-39). They returned to Rome and brought Christianity with them. Later, probably around 42 A.D., the Prince of the Apostles had come to Rome himself and, as the Fathers attest, organized this Church and became its head.

Since Paul had not met most of the Roman Christians, he introduces himself to them both as a person and an apostle: "Greetings from Paul, a servant of Christ Jesus, called to be an apostle and set apart to proclaim...the gospel concerning his Son...Jesus Christ Our Lord...that we may...bring to obedient faith all the Gentiles" (1:1, 3, 4, 5). As in the Letter to the Galatians, which Paul had written probably some months earlier, Paul sets forth his principle points of doctrine on man's justification by God through faith in Jesus Christ as opposed to the Mosaic Law. This law was "holy and just and good" (7:12), but "now we have been released from the law—for we have died to what bound us—and we serve in the new spirit, not the antiquated letter" (7:6). Romans is carefully planned. Its central theme is stated in 1:16-17: "I am not ashamed of the gospel. It is the power of God leading everyone who believes in it to salvation, the Jew first, then the Greek. For in the gospel is revealed the justice of God which begins and ends with faith; as Scripture says, 'The just man shall live by faith.' "

This letter is, therefore, more like a theological treatise than a letter, even though the reading of all Paul's other letters is necessary for acquiring a complete view of all his theological ideas. Romans contains a powerful exposition of the doctrine of the supremacy of Christ and of faith in Him as the only font of salvation

(3:21-26; 5:1-2, 8-11, 15-21). It is an implicit exhortation to the Christians of Rome to hold fast to their faith and to resist any pressure put on them to accept a doctrine of salvation through works alone.

St. Paul's teachings in the Letter to the Romans are saturated with the doctrine of grace (especially 5:15-19): its necessity and importance. It is grace that has saved us—not the value of our works (3:24-28).... The Mosaic Law was good and holy (7:12) because it really conveyed God's will to the Jews. But it could not give anyone the spiritual help necessary to obey it (8:3-4, 11-13). All it could do was to make people aware of sin and of the need they have of God's grace to help them (3:20; 7:7-13). All human beings need God's grace, and this is a gift from God. All human beings, united to Christ by faith and living the new life of grace by sharing the Spirit of Christ, are made perfect gratuitously (3:24) and so are enabled to live in the way God wants human beings to live (8:1-4). This faith must show in good works—not necessarily those commanded by the Mosaic Law, however, but works prompted by the Holy Spirit.

"The unspiritual are interested only in what is unspiritual," St. Paul states, "but the spiritual are interested in spiritual things.... So then, my brothers, there is no necessity for us to obey our unspiritual selves or to live unspiritual lives. If you do live in that way, you are doomed to die; but if by the Spirit you put an end to the misdeeds of the body you will live" (Rom. 8:5, 12-13).**

In the same letter, Paul vividly depicts the inner struggle which goes on within all human beings between the old Adam who perseveres within us, the flesh, and the higher aspirations of the soul. He concludes by saying that the higher aspirations gain victory through the grace of God, merited for mankind by Jesus Christ (7:14-25).

The Mosaic Law, which was the preparation for the coming of the Savior, has now served its purpose (7:6). (The Ten Commandments, of course, are an exception to this.) The Jews who insist upon the necessity of keeping the Law of Moses, St. Paul wrote, are putting themselves outside of the way of salvation (10:3-4). Because of this, the pagans have been invited in their place. However, Paul adds, this does not mean that God has cast off His people, the Jews. Their failure to live up to God's original choice will not be permanent; some of them, the "remnant," have already become believers, not by virtue of the works of the Law of Moses but out of grace. And one day most of them will become believers, as foretold by the prophets (chapters 9-11).

God's gift of salvation is for all (3:24); the whole human race is called to be children of God (8:14-17). The Christian, because of the Spirit's presence within him, enjoys a new life and a new relationship to God, "a spirit of adoption through which we cry out, 'Abba!' (that is, Father)" (Rom. 8:15). Therefore, St. Paul says, all Christians without exception—whether converted Jews or converted pagans—must love and help one another as children of God and members of one family, in humility and concord, in fraternal charity, in obedience to authority, in mutual patience, in peace, self-denial and reciprocal mercy (12—15:13).

STUDY QUESTIONS

1. *Who was St. Paul?*
2. *Why was the importance of the conversion of St. Paul extraordinary for the history of the Church and especially for us, children of the Gentiles?*
3. *What did St. Paul do?*
4. *What was St. Paul's basic teaching?*
5. *In what language did Paul write his letters?*
6. *When did St. Paul write his Letter to the Romans and why?*
7. *What does St. Paul set forth in his Letter to the Romans?*
8. *What theological ideas does St. Paul bring out in his Letter to the Romans?*

The First Letter of Paul to the Corinthians

On his second missionary journey, St. Paul preached for about two years at Corinth (50-52 A.D.), the capital city of Achaia in Greece—a great and populous city, a center of Hellenism, but also extremely immoral and dedicated to pagan cult.

Paul had chosen Corinth because it was a commercial city—a port with much traffic—and Paul hoped that the Christian faith would spread from there through all the nation. In Corinth, Paul made many converts, especially among the pagan poor (1 Cor. 1:26-28).

However, three to four years later a sort of crisis developed in Corinth. While in Ephesus, Paul was informed by members of the Corinthian Church of certain disorders in that Christian community: there were divisions (1:10-17), moral disorders (chapter 5) and public litigations (6:1-11), plus questions to be answered regarding marriage (7:1-24) and virginity (7:25-35), Eucharistic assemblies and other religious gatherings (10:14-33; 11:2-34) and charismatic gifts. Paul answers their questions sincerely and very practically, and corrects the disorders which have arisen. His masterful letter (written around 56 A.D.) reveals, almost like a journalistic report, a vivid picture of real-life Christians struggling to live their new Faith in an environment hostile to it in every way. His advice, given with clarity and authority, could have been written today, so similar is the present world to that of Corinth nearly 2000 years ago.

Paul wrote at least four letters to the Corinthians: one prior to the canonical First Corinthians (1 Cor. 5:9) and one afterwards, written "in great sorrow and anguish, with copious tears" (2 Cor. 2:4). The letter referred to in 1 Corinthians 5:9 has apparently not survived. Regarding the one mentioned in Second Corinthians, some scholars believe that 2 Corinthians 10 through 13 could perhaps be the letter of tears or at least part of it. There is a definite change of tone from chapters 1 through 9 to chapters 10 through 13, one of Paul's most severe passages. In any case, Pauline authorship of the letters known to us as First and Second Corinthians is undisputed. To read First Corinthians leads us to reflect with St. John Chrysostom: "Many err, many sin; remain with St. Paul and you will neither err nor sin."

For study questions, see page 188.

The Second Letter of Paul to the Corinthians

Paul wrote the Second Letter to the Corinthians from Macedonia (57 A.D.), during the course of his third missionary journey (Acts 20:1f.). He had previously sent Titus to Corinth to visit that community and to ascertain the effect on the faithful there of a severe letter which he had been obliged to write to them some time before (2:3ff.).

Following the good report given by Titus, Paul was greatly relieved and wrote the present Letter to the Corinthians. In it the Apostle shows his sufferings and consolations (1:3-11); his sincerity (1:12ff.); his honesty (1:15—2:4); his pardon for the offender (2:5-11); his past anxiety and present relief (2:12-17); his confidence in the apostolic ministry despite its hardships (3:1-6, 10); his desire for openheartedness on their part (6:11ff.; 7:2ff.); and his great love for them (7:2-16). He makes an appeal for the collection for the poor Christians in Jerusalem (8:1-9, 15). In the concluding chapters, 10 through 13, Paul gives a vigorous and rather severe defense of his ministry and mission as a true apostle of Jesus Christ. The marked change of tone in these chapters from the first part of the letter has led some scholars to believe that chapters 10 through 13 are part of the letter of rebuke written "with copious tears" and referred to in 2 Corinthians 2:4. Titus had been able to give Paul a good report on the beneficial effect of this letter. As a result Paul wrote the consoling words which are chapters 1 through 9 of "Second Corinthians." Paul concludes his defense with proofs of his sincerity and authority, amply attested by extraordinary visitations from heaven and by unparalleled labors and sufferings on behalf of the Gospel.

STUDY QUESTIONS

1. *When did St. Paul go to Corinth and what was Corinth like?*
2. *Why did St. Paul write his First Letter to the Corinthians and when did he write it?*
3. *When and where did St. Paul write his Second Letter to the Corinthians?*
4. *Why did he write his Second Letter to the Corinthians?*

The Letter of Paul to the Galatians

St. Paul's Letter to the Galatians was addressed to the Christians living in the highlands of modern Turkey. For centuries it was generally assumed that in his Letter to the Galatians, St. Paul wrote to Christian communities in Galatia proper, or simply the northern part of what was the Roman province of Galatia constituted by Octavian Augustus. For in 25 B.C., Augustus had constituted the province to include not only old Galatia but also Lycaonia, Pisidia, parts of Pamphylia and southern Phrygia. But St. Paul had founded communities in the north in his second missionary journey and visited them on his third. In this case the letter would have been written between the years 54 and 57 A.D.

But today many scholars hold that St. Paul in addressing the Galatians was addressing Christians in the southern part of Augustus' province. In this case St. Paul would have been addressing Churches founded in his first missionary journey and the letter would have been written shortly after that journey, around 48/49.

Although the Galatians had welcomed the Gospel with enthusiasm (4:14b-15), Judaizers from Jerusalem soon visited the new converts. These Judaizers insisted that the Gentiles could not be saved only by Baptism and faith in Christ, but also had to be circumcised (6:12-13) and observe the Mosaic Law (cf. 1:7; 2:3-5, 16).

The Judaizers also made light of St. Paul's apostolic authority. The news of this dangerous situation inflamed the fatherly heart of the Apostle with sadness and anger (1:6; 3:1, 3; 4:11, 16, 19-20). Paul was indignant not because his authority was being questioned—he was not concerned about his own self-esteem (1:10)—but because his children in the spirit were on the verge of losing the keystone of their Faith (2:21). The Judaizers' attack was on Christ Himself (5:21). Paul wrote this letter to vindicate his own authority (1:11—2:14) and to confront the seductions of the Judaizers with the true doctrine (2:16). This letter vibrates with Paul's character and fatherly love. His own words show how deeply their disloyalty stung his heart.

"I am amazed," he writes, "that you are so soon deserting him who called you in accord with his gracious design in Christ, and are going over to another gospel" (1:6). The fatherly sadness here elsewhere gives way to vehemence: "You senseless Galatians! ("Senseless"—in Greek, *anoetoi*, means imbeciles or persons completely lacking intelligence.) Who has cast a spell over you...?" (3:1)

In bold, vivid images, Paul strives to show them what they are doing. "God has sent forth into our hearts the spirit of his Son which cries out 'Abba!' ('Father!') You are no longer a slave but a son!... How can you return to those powerless, worthless, natural elements to which you seem willing to enslave yourselves once more? ...I fear for you; all my efforts with you may have been wasted!" (4:6, 9, 11)

The Letter to the Galatians is chiefly dogmatic, as is that to the Romans, and it defends the thesis that justification depends on faith in Christ rather than the Law of Moses. Following a brief prologue (1:1-10), the epistle consists of three parts. In the first (1:11—2:21), St. Paul shows that his doctrine is on a par with that of the other Apostles; in the second (3:1—4:31), he declares that for salvation faith in Christ is necessary, rather than the works of the Mosaic Law. The Law of Moses kept the Hebrews from falling into idolatry, gave them the principles of religion and morals, and guided them to Christ. Christ, with His death, freed man from the Law, making him die with Him and live of His same life (Romans, chapters 5, 6, 7, 8). Especially noteworthy is Paul's clear allegorical equation which connects Hagar with slavery and Sarah with freedom and the New Law

(4:21-31). In the third section (5:1—6:10), he gives practical advice to correct some abuses and strengthen his readers in the Faith. He concludes with an epilogue (6:11-18) which contains greetings and an invocation of God's blessings.

This letter gives a true image of St. Paul. It throbs with his energy, his fire, his zeal; it shows his power with words as well as his fatherly affection.

STUDY QUESTIONS

1. *When and to whom was this letter written?*
2. *How did the Galatians receive the Gospel message?*
3. *Why did St. Paul write this letter?*
4. *What is the theme of this letter?*
5. *How does this letter reveal St. Paul?*

The Letter of Paul to the Ephesians

Four letters are attributed to the time of Paul's first imprisonment in Rome (61-63 A.D.): Philippians, Colossians, Philemon and Ephesians. Of these "Captivity Letters," the Letter to the Ephesians is by far the most far-reaching in beauty and profound thought. The title "to the Ephesians" is misleading. These words (1:1) are missing from the two best early Greek manuscripts. This, coupled with the fact that Paul mentions no one by name (and he surely knew many individuals in this Church he had founded), have led most scholars to believe that here Paul is addressing all the Christians of the Roman province of Asia, in a sort of circular letter.

In the year 62-63 A.D. Paul learned that the faith of the flourishing Asian Churches, especially in the large centers, such as Ephesus, was being attacked by the heresy of Gnosticism. With his keen vision, Paul foresaw that this heresy would end in sacrilegious destruction of the great concepts of Jesus Christ as God and of the redemption through His blood. Thus, with flaming zeal, he dictated this Letter to the Ephesians and to the nearby Churches.

It seems that Paul wrote the Letter to the Ephesians soon after that to the Colossians. Ephesians, with its hymn of praise to the glorified Savior, amplifies the ideas exposed in Colossians.

The Church at Ephesus had been generated in Christ by Paul at the risk of his life. According to Acts (19:10) Paul stayed in Ephesus for two years so "that all the inhabitants of the province of Asia, Jews and Greeks alike, heard the word of the Lord" (Acts 19:10). From Ephesus further Churches sprang up: Colossae, Laodicea, Hierapolis. Paul was not directly the founder of these communities, which were as much as one hundred miles up the Lycus valley east of Ephesus. But he clearly felt the care of those disciples, as well as their Christian formation, depended wholly upon him.

Paul recalls to their minds the mystery of redemption through the blood of Christ (1:7), and their predestination as adopted sons of God (1:5). He praises God for "the glad tidings of salvation" (1:13) which, in Christ, are a blessing for Jew and Gentile alike. He raises his hands in grateful thanks for their belief and pictures a glorified Christ whom God raised "from the dead, seating him at his right hand in heaven, high above every principality, power, virtue, and domination, and every name that can be given in this age or in the age to come" (Eph. 1:20-21).

Almost exultantly he reflects on the secret call (3:3) of all nations to form the Mystical Body of Christ—the Church—"...so immeasurably generous is God's favor to us. God has given us the wisdom to understand fully the mystery, the plan he was pleased to decree in Christ, to be carried out in the fullness of time: namely, to bring all things in the heavens and on the earth into one under Christ's headship" (Eph. 1:8-10).

Paul says that Christ has made sinners to live again (2:5), that He is now our peace and our life (2:14), that this life is realized in the Church (1:19) in which we are reborn through Baptism. Christ is the Head of the Church, which is His Body and contains the fullness of His plenitude (1:22-23).

Christ, continues Paul, demolished the partition that separated the Hebrews and the rest of men, who were pagans or Gentiles (2:14). He called the Gentiles to the hope that was ancient Israel's, and in Christ he envisioned their unity (2:11-18). Paul illustrates this unity in another well-known figure of the Church: "You form a building which rises on the foundations of the apostles..." (2:20; cf. 19-22).

Because of this unity, the relations among the faithful of all classes *are* to be *marked* by perfect charity and brotherhood. Paul gives practical applications of unity in the Church. Christianity is a life in which the believer is made to live in Christ by the wonderful effects of grace. He encourages virtue in the members (4:1-6), harmony among those with a diversity of graces (4:7-17), and metanoia in every area of life (4:17—5:21). It is a life that is not limited to domestic walls or to the bosom of the Church. Christianity is a life entailing a series of obligations towards all classes of people, a life that embraces all the hours of the day, all the thoughts of the mind, all the actions of the body. It excludes nothing but sin.

Paul then gives specific advice on Christian family life (5:21—6:9) and concludes with a comparison of Christian life to spiritual warfare (6:10-17). With a recommendation to constant prayer, he humbly asks for prayers for himself "that I may courageously make known the mystery of the gospel" (Eph. 6:19).

In concluding his letter, Paul recommends courage and perseverance, exhorting each person to prepare himself to resist the powers of hell by practicing virtue, prayer and good works.

STUDY QUESTIONS

1. *When was this letter written?*
2. *What is the reason this letter was written?*
3. *What are the main points of this letter?*
4. *What are Paul's recommendations?*
5. *Which letter is Ephesians linked with? Why?*

The Letter of Paul to the Philippians

Philippi was the first European city to be evangelized by St. Paul. Founded by Philip II, father of Alexander the Great, it was elevated by Augustus to the status of a Roman colony and enjoyed special rights and privileges. Paul preached the Gospel there during his second missionary journey; he revisited the city twice on his third journey—in the fall of 57 A.D. and the spring of 58 A.D. (Acts 20:1-6).

The Christians of Philippi were always very devoted to St. Paul and frequently sent him offerings (4:10-18; 2 Cor. 11:9). This letter was written from prison (1:7) and expresses the Apostle's gratitude for a generous offering that Epaphroditus had brought him in their name (4:10, 14, 18).

He offers consolation to those who share sufferings with him for the sake of Christ (1:29, 30). Paul thanks God for the Philippians' loyalty to him and to the Gospel "continually...from the very first day" (Phil. 1:5).

The style of the letter is cordially conversational, rather than didactic. Paul warns the Philippians against some "bad workmen" (Phil. 3:2) who are trying to ruin what he has built up elsewhere. He urges them to be united, humble and persevering. While making this appeal, he writes—or quotes—a hymn that reflects the early Church's strong faith in Christ's divinity:

"Your attitude must be that of Christ:

> Though he was in the form of God,
>   he did not deem equality with God
>   something to be grasped at.

> Rather, he emptied himself
> and took the form of a slave,
> being born in the likeness of men..." (Phil. 2:5-7).

This letter gives us a sense of St. Paul's great love for the Philippians. It is a letter of Christian hope and fatherly tenderness, in which expressions of gratitude alternate with wise counsels.

Philippians is believed to have been written either from Ephesus around 56 or 57 A.D., or from Rome in 62 or 63 A.D.

STUDY QUESTIONS

1. When was this letter written?
2. What is the style and message of this letter?
3. What does this letter portray?

The Letter of Paul to the Colossians

The Christian community of Colossae, a town about 100 miles east of Ephesus, was founded by Epaphras, who was probably one of Paul's Ephesian converts. The Apostle took a personal interest in the work of his disciple (2:1). A few years later, while Paul was under arrest, he had news of the Colossians through Epaphras. Though the report of the evangelist was, on the whole, favorable (1:4-8; 2:5f.), he saw dangerous tendencies in the young Christian community. Vain speculations borrowed from various pagan cults about celestial or cosmic powers thought to control the universe preoccupied some Colossians. In some Jewish circles these powers were interpreted as angels, and there seemed to be a possibility that these were usurping Christ's power (2:18f.). Others, who boasted of a deeper knowledge of Christianity, insisted on Judaic observances (2:16) and a false asceticism (2:20-23). Concerned lest his work be destroyed, Epaphras had come to Rome to seek help from Paul.

Paul met the danger by sending a letter to Colossae, borne by Tychicus and Onesimus (4:7-9). To counter the error of the false teachers, he set forth in clear terms the true doctrine concerning Christ, our God (1:19; 2:9) and Redeemer, Head of the Mystical Body, the Church (1:15—2:3), and drew up rules for an ideal Christian life (3:5—4:6). Between these positive sections, the Apostle inserted a vigorous condemnation of the false teachings (2:4—3:4). Because of the emphatic statement of Christ's divinity that they contain, the first two chapters of the letter are of great doctrinal importance.

As mentioned previously the Epistle to the Colossians bears a remarkable resemblance to the Epistle to the Ephesians. Most of the words and phrases of this shorter letter are met with in the other also. Written at the same time, both were addressed to communities of Jewish and pagan converts, struggling in like circumstances to maintain the purity of their Faith.

STUDY QUESTIONS

1. What errors infiltrated among the young Christian community?
2. What message does this letter contain?
3. Which parts of this letter are particularly important? Why?
4. What letter of St. Paul is similar to this? Why?

The First Letter of Paul to the Thessalonians

St. Paul founded the Church at Thessalonica during the early part of his second great missionary journey in the summer of 50 A.D. Thessalonica, the capital of Macedonia, was a large and important city. Its population was predominantly Gentile, but Jews dwelt there in sufficient numbers to have a synagogue. Paul succeeded in converting some of the Jews and a large number of Gentiles. But his success stirred up the hostility of some unbelieving Jews, who by calumny and riot compelled him to flee to Beroea. From there he went to Athens and Corinth, and it was in the latter city that this letter was written (winter of 50-51 A.D.). It is the earliest of all the New Testament books.

While at Athens, Paul, fearing lest the persecution which continued against the Christians of Thessalonica should cause his new converts to abandon the Faith, had sent Timothy to ascertain conditions in the Church and to comfort and strengthen that community (3:1-8). Timothy reported to Paul at Corinth, bringing the good news of their constancy in the face of persecution. He likewise informed Paul that the Thessalonians required further instruction on the resurrection of the dead and the second coming of Christ.

Paul begins his letter with deep gratitude for their strong faith under trial (1:2-3, 6) and an expression of his satisfaction for their firm adherence to the Gospel (2:14ff.), "a model for all the believers of Macedonia and Achaia" (1 Thes. 1:7). He exhorts them to grow in holiness (3:9-13) and to live in chastity and charity (4:1-12). Paul then answers their questions about those who have died, their resurrection and the second coming of Christ (4:13-18). He concludes with a counsel to be prepared for the Lord, "awake and sober" (1 Thes. 5:6), especially by leading upright Christian lives (5:12-19).

STUDY QUESTIONS

1. *When was the Church of Thessalonica founded?*
2. *When and why was this letter written?*
3. *How does Paul begin his letter?*
4. *Who was sent to the Christians of Thessalonica by Paul and why?*

The Second Letter of Paul to the Thessalonians

Most scholars believe that this letter was written by Paul from Corinth a short time after the first one and it is like the continuation and complement of the first. In it, the Apostle praises the Christians of Thessalonica because their faith, peace and constancy increase under persecution (1:3-10), and he prays for their progress (1:11-12). He especially repeats that the community's life is not to be guided by the false belief that the second coming of Christ was at hand.

Some among them had ceased to work for a living (in view of the supposed imminence of the parousia), and consequently had to depend upon others for sustenance (3:6-10). Paul tells the Thessalonians to refuse to support them gratuitously and even to gradually but firmly exclude them from the community (3:14). He concludes this section with these fatherly words: "If anyone refuses to obey what I have written in this letter, take note of him and have nothing to do with him, so that he will feel that he is in the wrong; though you are not to regard him as an enemy but as a brother in need of correction" (2 Thes. 3:14-15).**

STUDY QUESTIONS

1. *How does this letter compare with the first and what is its message?*
2. *What is Paul's recommendation?*

The Letters of Paul to Timothy and Titus

These three letters of Paul—two to Timothy and one to Titus—have been referred to as the "pastoral letters" since the 18th century. All of them are very similar in substance, form and historical background. Paul wrote them to two of his closest collaborators (Acts 16:1ff.; 2 Cor 2:13ff.) to instruct them on the organization and administration of the Churches entrusted to their pastoral care. Timothy was originally from Lystra in Lycaonia, where Paul personally selected the young man to be his companion. Timothy later became bishop of the Church in Ephesus. Titus, a Gentile convert of Paul and so the Apostle's "own true child in our common faith" (Ti. 1:4), was left in Crete to "accomplish what had been left undone, especially the appointment of presbyters in every town" (Ti. 1:5).

The First Letter to Timothy and that to Titus seem to have been written from Macedonia at approximately the same time (around 65 A.D.). Their contents and instructions bear a close resemblance. Second Timothy, on the other hand, seems to have been written later, possibly shortly before Paul's death in 67 A.D. His words indicate captivity and a premonition of death: "I for my part am already being poured out like a libation. The time of my dissolution is near" (2 Tm. 4:6; cf. also 2 Tm. 1:12).

Paul, like someone about to go away for a long time, entrusts to his young helpers what is most precious to him—the deposit of Faith (1 Tm. 1:10, 6:20; 2 Tm. 1:14). He charges them repeatedly to preserve it from false doctrines (1 Tm. 1:3, etc.). He enumerates the qualities and duties of various ministers (indicating a hierarchy) and pictures many of the difficulties and problems of the early Church. The pastoral directives Paul sets down also make the letters valuable handbooks even today for ministers of the Church and all who work with them.

Paul begins his First Letter to Timothy by greeting the young bishop and reminding him of the duty to warn the faithful against false doctrines (chapter 1). In fighting the good fight (1:18) Timothy must instruct the Christians in prayer and proper conduct (chapter 2). Paul's reference to the position of women in the assemblies answered a need for regulation.

Rev. J. Kingsley Dalpadado, O.M.I., offers the following observation in his informative book, *Reading the Acts, Epistles and Revelation* (St. Paul Editions):

"In this particular Christian community, some women seem to have been a problem. The injunctions given...are best understood in the light of the cultural background, Jewish and Hellenistic, which seemed to merge and even clash in the Churches of Asia Minor and Greece. (In the Jewish synagogues, women had no active part in the public worship, whereas in the pagan Greek world women played a major part as priestesses and prophetesses.) In the present salvific moment, one must remember that Paul is here writing a *letter,* not a theological treatise or dogmatic statement regarding women. He is giving particular directions to a particular situation at a particular time."

Paul proceeds to set down qualifications for the various ministers (chapter 3), rules for widows (5:3-16), and practical pastoral advice (chapters 4, 5, 6). He closes with a further plea for Timothy to be steadfast in the Faith.

The Second Letter to Timothy, written during Paul's final captivity, is the Apostle's last will and testament to his beloved son in the Lord. Together with personal news (2 Tm. 1:11-18), Paul gives Timothy an exhortation to courage and perseverance (1:6-10). He urges him to face difficulties after Christ's example and his own (2:1-13; 10:14); he reminds the young bishop to live up to his vocation and carry out his ministry with dedication (4:1-5). Most precious is the clear affirmation of Scripture's divine inspiration contained in 3:16-17.

This letter ends with a lengthy conclusion in which Paul declares his readiness to lay down his life as a sacrifice to God (4:6-7) and expresses a quiet hope that the Lord will stand by him in all trials and bring him safely to His heavenly kingdom (4:8, 18).

The third pastoral letter is addressed to Titus. Titus accompanied Paul and Barnabas to the Council of Jerusalem (Gal. 2:1) and went with Paul on his third missionary journey. From this letter we learn that St. Paul had entrusted Titus with the organization of the Christian community in Crete through the appointment of presbyters (1:5). Because of the character of the inhabitants (1:12) and the spread of erroneous doctrines (1:10-11), Titus' task was a difficult one. In this epistle the Apostle gives him advice and instructions (2:1-15; 3:8-15) to guide him in his episcopal office. He also gives various counsels for fostering the Christian life of the faithful (3:1-8).

STUDY QUESTIONS

1. *What other name is given to these three letters? Why?*
2. *Who were Timothy and Titus?*
3. *What is contained in the First Letter to Timothy?*
4. *What is Paul's concept of women according to this letter?*
5. *What is the message in Second Timothy?*
6. *How does this letter end?*
7. *What do we learn from Paul's Letter to Titus?*

The Letter of Paul to Philemon

Paul wrote this warm note to Philemon, a wealthy convert of the Church of Colossae. It is a request for mercy on one of Philemon's runaway slaves, Onesimus, formerly lazy (v. 11) and addicted to stealing (v. 17). Probably written in Paul's own hand, the letter implores Philemon to "receive [Onesimus] as a brother" (cf. v. 16)—a rather revolutionary concept for those times. Paul had met Onesimus in Rome, taken him in instead of turning him over to the authorities, and led him to belief in the Gospel. Now Paul was returning him to his master and asking that he be treated like another Paul (v. 17).

Though only a short twenty verses, this letter expresses in concise terms the Pauline doctrine of the dignity of the Christian and of the love that Christians should have for one another by reason of their union in Christ. Paul does not attack the social institution of slavery, which the small Christian communities were in no position to alter within a dictatorial political structure. But he solves the problem by applying *Christian principles* to the relations that should exist between master and slave—the two should remember that they are brothers who serve the same Master (v. 16; Col. 3:22; 4:1). This approach to social problems is a valid one for all times.

STUDY QUESTIONS

1. *Why did Paul write this letter?*
2. *What concise terms are met with in this letter?*

The Letter to the Hebrews

Although from early times Hebrews was included among the letters of St. Paul, many of today's scholars point out literary characteristics which they feel are quite different from those of the Apostle of the Gentiles. However, the letter has such strong Pauline overtones that scholars feel Paul had a great deal of influence on the writer. They suggest that Paul made use of a secretary to whom he gave great freedom, being content to simply pen the closing lines himself (13:22-25). Some think that the author of Hebrews was a person very familiar with Paul's doctrine and quite fluent as regards Old Testament Scriptures—perhaps Luke, or Apollos.

The central theme of this masterful letter is the high-priesthood of Christ, He who is more exalted than the angels, faithful and compassionate (chapters 3-5), and whose office and sacrifice are eternal (5:11—10:39).

The date of the Letter is uncertain, but it could be ascribed to the period around the destruction of the Temple.

The Letter to the Hebrews bears a message of encouragement plainly directed to Judaeo-Christians who were thoroughly familiar with the Old Testament and with all the ceremonies of the Temple. Some have even suggested that they were possibly Jewish priest-converts, who had fled from Jerusalem because of persecution and now longed for the beautiful pageantry of Temple worship. The community was apparently in a period of difficulty at the time "Hebrews" was written, possibly connected with a temptation to return to Judaism. The author of Hebrews intends to prevent just this. He argues skillfully from Scripture itself and from the perfection of Christ's sacrifice (10:19-39) to convincingly show that the New Covenant completes and fully realizes the Old, which "has become obsolete and has grown old...close to disappearing" (Heb. 8:13). To embrace Judaism once again would be to embrace a mere shadow.

This letter may be described as a brief apologetic for Christianity.

After a solemn prologue (1:1-4), the author treats: the superiority of Christ (1:5—2:18); Christ's characteristics as high priest (3:1—4:13); the priesthood and victimhood of Christ (5:1—10:18); the necessity of both faith and works (10:19—13:19).

By illustrating the excellence of Christ's sacrifice and high priesthood (7:26-28), His power (1:5-14) and exaltation (2:5-18), the author draws the forceful conclusion of the consequent impotence of the Old Covenant (8:7-13). He further warns of the terrible results if one were to apostatize and return to the dying testament, thus falling "into the hands of the living God" (Heb. 10:31).

It is necessary, he emphasizes, to keep one's faith in Christ, who by God's will has become the sole cause of our salvation (3:14; 7:28; 9:14, 28, etc.).

Through His priestly work, Christ has opened a way for us to heaven through His death on the cross, the author tells us. Let us walk in this way with hearts filled with faith, firm in hope, responsive in love (10:19-25).

Undiscouraged by the troubles they have so far endured, Christians must look forward to the great reward that is to come soon (10:32-39).

In the concluding chapters, the author cites examples of faith from the Old Testament (chapter 11), and explains that God often uses trials to train His children (chapter 12): "For whom the Lord loves, he disciplines; he scourges every son he receives" (Heb. 12:6). He recalls the penalties of disobedience, and concludes with a final exhortation and blessing to the readers (chapter 13).

The blood of Jesus assures our entrance into the sanctuary by the new and living path He has opened up for us through the veil (the "veil" meaning His flesh) (10:19). Let us thank and praise God for this all the days of our life.

Thus, rather than let ourselves be discouraged by difficulties or dangers, we should imitate the patriarchs and other faithful believers who held to the right course despite sufferings and even death itself. "Remember your leaders who spoke the word of God to you; consider how their lives ended and imitate their faith. Jesus Christ is the same yesterday, today, and forever" (Heb. 13:7-8).

STUDY QUESTIONS

1. *What is the central theme of this letter?*
2. *What particular message is seen in this letter?*
3. *What is the author's intention for writing this letter?*
4. *How can this letter be described?*
5. *What is denounced by the author?*
6. *How is this letter divided?*

The Letter of James

The author of this letter is usually identified with that James, called the "brother of the Lord," who was the leader of the Judaeo-Christian community in Jerusalem (Acts 12:17ff; 15:13-21; 21:18-26; 1 Cor. 15:7; Gal. 1:19; 2:9, 12). He was martyred in 62 A.D. by the Jews. Even though probably not an Apostle, his letter was accepted from the beginning as having authority. The exact date of his writing is uncertain, but internal evidence points to the year 57 A.D., although it could have been as early as 49 A.D.

The letter is addressed "to the twelve tribes in the dispersion" (Jas. 1:1), that is, to the Judaeo-Christians living outside Jerusalem and all over the Greco-Roman world. Because of this universal thrust, and the absence of any specific community's name, this letter, along with the three of John, two of Peter and one of Jude, make up the body of "catholic" or "universal" epistles, so named since the end of the 2nd century.

The Letter of James is remarkable for its eminently practical character, which applies the spirit of the Sermon on the Mount to daily life. With a special predilection for the poor (1:9-11; 1:27—2:9; 4:13—5:6), he echoes the Old Testament tradition of God's favored ones (anawim), but especially reflects the beatitudes (Mt. 5:3ff.) and Jesus' attitude toward the poor.

The author, in developing his second theme, insists that we cannot be saved by knowledge but rather by the exercise of the Christian virtues. As followers of Christ, we cannot be satisfied with a faith that produces nothing (1:22-27; 2:10-26). The author stresses social justice, champions the rights of the poor and urges that faith be shown through good works—without which, he declares, faith "is as dead as a body without breath" (Jas. 2:26).

Besides these two themes, James also deals with several other subjects in his forceful style: Christian conduct in times of suffering (1:1-12; 5:7-11); the origin of temptation (1:13-18); keeping one's tongue in check (1:26; 3:1-18); treatment of our neighbor (2:8, 13; 3:13—4:2; 4:11f.); and the power of prayer (1:5-8; 4:2f.; 5:13-18) which includes the classical reference for the sacrament of the Anointing of the Sick (5:14ff.).

Its incisiveness and practicality make this letter very fruitful reading in every age.

STUDY QUESTIONS

1. *Why is the Letter of James also called "catholic"?*
2. *Why is the Letter of James remarkable?*
3. *What is stressed in this letter?*

The First Letter of Peter

We are reading now the Letter of St. Peter the Apostle, *the first Pope,* addressed to the Church at large.

After the incident recounted in the twelfth chapter of Acts, the Prince of the Apostles, the Vicar of Christ, left Jerusalem "to go off to another place" (Acts 12:17). Having preached at Jerusalem as first in the apostolic college, he also preached in Antioch for some time. He eventually went to Rome where, as first Bishop of the Church there, he preached the Gospel until the end of his life. Tradition tells us that he was martyred there on June 29, in the year 67 A.D.

There has never been any question of Peter's authorship of this letter, even though he had Silvanus as his secretary (5:12), who had also assisted Paul. Peter wrote the letter from Rome (which he called "Babylon," 5:13) between 63 and 65 A.D.

This first Letter of Peter reflects a time of trial through which the Church was passing because of the persecution of Nero. It contains much practical teaching under the dominating theme of fortitude in trial, for which Christ Himself is the model (4:1, 13, etc.). And yet, "First Peter" is also a valuable synthesis of apostolic theology.

It is addressed to the Christian communities of five provinces which comprise practically all of Asia Minor, to whom St. Peter had probably preached. Such communities were, for the most part, composed of converts from paganism, although the Jewish element was not lacking.

The letter's simple and practical doctrine, expressed with sublime gravity, encourages in affliction, strengthens faith, and preaches the necessity of good works for eternal salvation.

St. Peter was a practical man who knew how to produce in a few words a masterpiece of wisdom and edification, infusing into his writing all the enthusiasm and generosity typical of his character, perhaps unpolished, but constant and ardent with love.

For study questions, see page 213.

The Second Letter of Peter

Although there is some discussion regarding actual authorship of this letter, the Church has accepted it as canonical (i.e., a true part of the inspired Word of God), and as an authentic document deriving from apostolic times.

The main object of the Second Letter of Peter is the refutation of false doctrines spread by false prophets (2:1) who were, in addition, leading dissolute lives (2:2). It is an urgent exhortation to faith and love of God (3:11-15) by reminding the faithful that although the second coming of the Lord had been delayed, He would indeed return in glory (3:9-10).

Interesting to note also is the letter's reference that Christians are "sharers of the divine nature" (1:4), as well as a clear statement on the inspiration of Scripture (1:20-21). The reminder "to be on your guard" (3:17) while we await the "new heavens and a new earth" (3:13) is as actual and pertinent to us in our times as it was to the original readers.

STUDY QUESTIONS

1. *When was the First Letter of Peter written and what does it reflect?*
2. *What teachings does this letter contain?*
3. *Why is this letter valuable?*
4. *What is the main object of the Second Letter of Peter?*
5. *What is recommended in this letter?*

The First Letter of John

Who is Jesus? St. John the Apostle, a witness to the historical Christ, can tell us. With St. Peter and St. James, John lived in very close contact with Jesus. These three Apostles witnessed His transfiguration on Tabor and His agony in Gethsemane. John was the only Apostle privileged to rest his head on Christ's heart, and he was the only one with the courage to follow the Master publicly during His passion. He saw Jesus die on Calvary. With the other Apostles, he also witnessed His resurrection and ascension into heaven.

St. John's literary witness to Christ includes the three canonical letters ascribed to him. The first letter is a summary of the fourth Gospel, and is the most important of the three. It was probably written last, around the same time as the Gospel, in the form of a circular letter to the Churches of Asia.

In this letter he was already concerned about rising heresies denying the divinity of Jesus Christ (2:18, 22f.). He refuted these errors and affirmed that Christ is truly God (2:23) and truly man (4:2); the Victim (2:1-2); the source of grace and forgiveness (2:12; 5:16); the Mediator, who communicates life (3:11-12), light and truth.

So it is that the basic themes of this First Letter of St. John are the divinity of Jesus Christ and the revelation of God's love for man. God is love, John tells us, and He sent His Son as an offering for our sins.

"Beloved,
if God has loved us so,
we must have the same love for one another" (1 Jn. 4:11).

"The commandment we have from him is this:
whoever loves God must also love his brother"
(1 Jn. 4:21).

For Study Questions, see page 215.

The Second and Third Letters of John

The second canonical letter ascribed to John is addressed to "a Lady who is elect and to her children." However, scholars assume from its contents that the Lady is a Church rather than an individual. It is a short, conventional note in which the "elder" (2 Jn. v. 1), as the author calls himself, encourages this community to show its Christianity by growing in faith (2 Jn. v. 9), charity (2 Jn. v. 5), and zeal, and by adhering to the truth about Jesus, avoiding those who deny the reality of His incarnation (2 Jn. v. 7f.).

In the third letter, the "elder" praises Gaius for his true practice of Christianity by giving hospitality and support to missionaries sent by the "elder" (3 Jn. vv. 5-8). It also condemns the ambition of a certain Diotrephes, who rejects the elder's authority (3 Jn. v. 9). He recommends, instead, Demetrius, who witnessed to the truth that was in him (3 Jn. v. 12).

STUDY QUESTIONS

1. Who is the author of the First Letter of John?
2. What is the theme of John's first letter?
3. What is the message of the Second and Third Letters of John?
4. To whom are these letters addressed?

The Letter of Jude

The author of this letter identifies himself as "Jude, the brother of James," and, so, also a cousin of the Lord (cf. Mt. 13:55ff.), though not the Apostle of the same name. Jude, who wrote the letter between 70 and 80 A.D. intended to denounce the false teachers who constituted a danger to Christian faith (vv. 3, 4). These false brethren rejected Christ, led lives that were openly immoral (vv. 8, 10, 13, 19), and lacked respect for authority (v. 16). The author threatens them with the divine punishment. He warns against these sensualists, who, "devoid of the Spirit, are causing divisions" (v. 19). He exhorts Christians to maintain a correct attitude and live a good life, so that they can overcome the situation by the power of God's grace (vv. 20-25).

From time to time, history repeats itself in the Church and in the world. Jude's warnings teach us also to be always on our guard.

STUDY QUESTIONS

1. *What is the purpose of this letter?*
2. *What is the warning given in this letter?*

The Book of Revelation

In the Greek, this book is called the Apocalypse of John. It belongs to the type of writing called *apocalyptic*, which means that it treats of a revelation from God regarding things that are hidden—especially future events.

The author of Revelation states that his name is John (1:9) and that he has written the book while in exile on the island of Patmos. Though some question whether the author is John the Apostle, their arguments seem inconclusive.

According to the most common opinion, the time of writing was during the reign of a fierce persecutor, the Emperor Domitian (81-96 A.D.), and many scholars suggest 95 A.D. as a probable date.

The Book of Revelation may be divided into seven principal sections: prologue (1:1-3), letters to the Churches of Asia (1:4—3:22), preparation for the Day of the Lord (4:1—16:21), the punishment of Babylon (17:1—19:10), the destruction of the pagan nations (19:11—20:15), the new creation (21:1—22:5), epilogue (22:6-21).

The Book of Revelation is richly symbolic, and this characteristic should be kept in mind. As in poetry, this book often contracts time and events, and uses figures, metaphors, and especially great fullness of expression. Events far removed from one another in time, as well as dissimilar facts are condensed in eternity.

In apocalyptic writing, almost everything—whether number or color, person or place, object or action—stands for something else. Here, for example, "the Beast" and "Babylon" represent persecuting Rome; horns mean power; eyes signify knowledge; the number 1,000 symbolizes immensity.

Also, the Book of Revelation is to be viewed as a tract for its own era, which was a period of disturbance and bitter persecution. Like the Old Testament Book of Daniel, which it somewhat resembles, Revelation was written to increase the hope and courage of God's people. Yet its message is valid for us, too, and for Christians of all time. The Church must always undergo suffering yet Christ will be with her until the end of the ages as He promised. Those who stand fast with Him will be victorious. The Book of Revelation is the persecuted Church's hymn of triumph.

STUDY QUESTIONS

1. *To what type of writing does this book belong?*
2. *When was this book written?*
3. *List the sections that this book can be divided into.*
4. *What should be kept in mind when reading the Book of Revelation?*

Bible Passages for Particular Needs

When you are sad
    read: Psalm 34; John 14; Matthew 6:19-34; Philippians 4

When your friends fail you
    read: Psalm 27; Matthew 10; Luke 17; Romans 12

When there is sin
    read: Psalm 51; Luke 15

Before worship in church
    read: Psalm 84

When you are in danger
    read: Psalms 21, 91; Matthew 11:25-30; Luke 8:22-25; 2 Timothy 3

When God seems to be very far away
    read: Psalm 139; Philippians 4:6-9; 1 Peter 5:7; Matthew 6:25-34

When you are discouraged
    read: Psalm 23; Isaiah 40; Matthew 5:4; 1 John 3:1-3

When you wish to produce good fruits (good results—succeed)
    read: John 15

When doubts assail you
    read: John 7:17; Luke 11:1-3

When you are alone and afraid
    read: Psalms 22, 42:6-11; Hebrews 13:5

When you need interior peace
    read: Psalm 85; Luke 10:38-42; Romans 5:1-5 Colossians 3:15

When you need prayer
> read: Psalms 4, 6, 25, 42; Matthew 6:5-15; Luke 11:1-3; John 17

When you are ill and in pain
> read: Psalms 38, 41:2-4; 91; Matthew 26:39; Romans 5:3-5; Hebrews 12:1-11; James 5:11-15

In temptation
> read: Matthew 6:24; Mark 9:42; Luke 21:33-36; Romans 13:13; James 1:12; Jude 24:25

In affliction
> read: Psalms 16, 31, 34, 37, 38, 40, 139; Matthew 11:28-30; John 14:1-4

In weariness
> read: Psalms 6, 27, 90; Matthew 11:28-30; Galatians 6:9, 10

In thanksgiving
> read: Psalms 65, 84, 92, 96, 100, 103, 116, 136, 147; 1 Thessalonians 5:18; Hebrews 13:15

In joy
> read: Philippians 4; Psalms 97, 99; Luke 1:46-56

Special Psalms for Special Needs

When tired or upset
    read: Psalm 4

When discouraged
    read: Psalm 42

When persecuted
    read: Psalm 36

When alone or disillusioned by a friend
    read: Psalm 40

When tempted to trust in oneself
    read: Psalm 51

When scared by a storm
    read: Psalm 29

When filled with great happiness
    read: Psalms 97, 99

When truly repentant
    read: Psalm 51

When grateful for the gifts of God
    read: Psalm 135

When in need of refuge
    read: Psalm 46

When in danger
    read: Psalm 91

When life needs a spiritual boost
    read: Psalm 27

When ready to travel
    read: Psalm 121

When worried
    read: Psalm 34

When anguished in life
　　read: Psalms 31, 34

When in need of confidence, of courage
　　read: Psalms 27, 31, 56, 62

When in need of health
　　read: Psalms 6, 27, 39, 41

When tempted
　　read: Psalms 46, 56, 131

Bibliography

Ahern, B., et al., ed. *New Testament Reading Guide* (series of pamphlets). Collegeville, MN: The Liturgical Press.

Albright, W. *The Archaeology of Palestine*. London: Penguin Books, 1949.

Brown, R., et al., ed. *The Jerome Biblical Commentary*. Englewood Cliffs, NJ: Prentice-Hall, Inc., 1968.

Dalpadado, K. *Reading the Bible*. Boston: St. Paul Editions, 1973.

_____ *Reading the Gospels*. Boston: St. Paul Editions, 1976.

Danielou, J. *The Dead Sea Scrolls and Primitive Christianity*. New York: New American Library, 1962.

Daniel-Rops, H. *Israel and the Ancient World*. London: Longmans, 1949.

_____ *Jesus and His Times*. London: Burns & Oates, 1955.

_____ *What Is the Bible?* New York: Guild Press, 1960.

Fuller, R., et al., ed. *A New Catholic Commentary on Holy Scripture*. Nashville, TN: Thomas Nelson, Inc., 1975.

Garofalo, S., ed. *La Sacra Bibbia*. Italy: Marietti Ed., Ltd., 1960.

Grollenberg, L. *Atlas of the Bible*. London: Thomas Nelson, Ltd., 1956.

Hardon, J. *Modern Catholic Dictionary*. Garden City, NY: Doubleday & Co., Inc., 1980.

Harrington, W. *Key to the Bible* (3 vols.). Canfield, OH: Alba House Communications, 1974.

Heidt, W., et al., ed. *Old Testament Reading Guide* (series of pamphlets). Collegeville, MN: The Liturgical Press.

Jones, A., et al., ed. *The Jerusalem Bible*. Garden City, NY: Doubleday & Co., Inc., 1966.

Knox, R., trans., *The Holy Bible*. New York: Sheed and Ward, Inc., 1956.

Moriarty, F. *Foreword to the Old Testament Books*. Weston, MA: Weston College Press, 1964.

Murphy, R. *The Dead Sea Scrolls and the Bible*. Westminster, MD: The Newman Press, 1957.

Robaldo, G., et al., ed. *Sacra Bibbia*. Rome: Edizioni Paoline, 1958.

Robert, A. *Guide to the Bible*. Westminster, MD: Newman Press, 1955.

Vermes, G. *The Dead Sea Scrolls in English*. London: Penguin Books, 1975.

_____ *The Dead Sea Scrolls: Qumran in Perspective*. Cleveland: Collins-World, 1978.

The Contemporary New Testament Series

EACH BOOKLET: 8½" × 11" — 32 pages
22 BOOKLETS PLUS INDEXES

"The introductory material, the historical outlines, articles on Biblical questions besides explanations of Biblical persons, places and terms—all combine to enhance the modern, up-to-date and faithful English translation of Sacred Scripture.
"For home and classroom, Bible discussion and adult education programs, this series will prove an invaluable aid."

Rev. Stephen J. Hartdegen, OFM
Editor-in-chief of the New American Bible

A WONDERFULLY INNOVATIVE WAY TO STUDY THE NEW TESTAMENT

...individually or in religion classes (senior high schools, colleges, seminaries), study groups, adult religion courses....

Complete New Testament text of the New American Bible.

Clear, up-to-date articles by noted Biblical scholars such as Bouyer, Charlier, Crisolit, Cullman, Danielou, Frossard, Harrington, Goldstain, on:

—History and physical description of New Testament regions and cities: Jerusalem, Patmos, Ephesus, etc.
—Origins of the various Books of the New Testament
—Discussion of authors' styles and purposes

—Explanation of special passages or doctrinal problems
—Answers to questions frequently asked
—Glossary of persons, places and terms

Plus in-depth explanatory captions of great educational value.

Discover the Awesome Beauty and Power of the Word of God

Each issue contains photographs of Biblical sites and scenes as they look today; museum art pieces such as paintings, miniatures, sculptures, bas-reliefs; architectural ruins relating to the New Testament.

1   **THE GOSPELS** (issues 1-11 plus index)
$1.20 per issue; index — 50¢

The eleven issues of the Gospels with index can be ordered as an entire set or individual Gospels can be ordered separately:
1 set of Matthew—booklets 1, 2, 3; 1 set of Mark—booklets 4, 5; 1 set of Luke—booklets 6, 7, 8; 1 set of John—booklets 9, 10, 11.

2   **ACTS, LETTERS, AND REVELATION** (issues 12-22 plus index) $1.20 per issue; index — 50¢

The eleven issues are divided as follows:
Acts—booklets 12, 13, 14; Letters—booklets 15, 16, 17, 18, 19, 20; Revelation—booklets 21 and 22.

Please order from addresses at the end of this book.

Three handy-sized, *pictorial abridgements of the SCRIPTURES*

Compiled with explanatory and introductory notes by Biblical scholars under the direction of Msgr. E. Galbiati.

Revised Standard Version—Catholic Edition—used throughout.

Each volume presents:

—Maps of the place in which the event may have occurred as well as short notes explaining the text.
—Full-color, full-page photographs of the places or objects referred to in the Biblical passages.

The History of Salvation in THE OLD TESTAMENT

CONTENTS
Introduction
- Revelation and the Bible
- The Books of the Bible
- The Geography of the Bible
- The Historical Background of the Bible

A Span of 10 Periods
- The Beginnings
- The Patriarchs
- The Exodus
- Joshua and the Judges
- The Beginnings of the Monarchy
- David and Solomon
- The Two Kingdoms
- The Exile and Expectation of the Kingdom of God
- The Faith of the Returned Exiles
- The Maccabees

Indexes

466 pages; $4.00 — SC0420

The Unified Text of the Gospel THE GOSPEL OF JESUS

...unfolds the story of Jesus in a most appealing and practical way for all age groups.

CONTENTS
Geographical and Historical Introduction
- Geography of Palestine in the time of our Lord
- Political and religious situation
- The Temple and the Jewish priesthood
- Measurement of time among the Jews
- Jewish festivals
- Chronology of the life of Jesus
- The origin of the four Gospels
- The Books of the Old and New Testaments

Reader's Guide
The Gospel of Jesus
- The infancy and hidden life
- Public ministry of Jesus
- The passion and death
- The resurrection and appearances of Jesus

Index

382 pages; $3.80 — SC0040

The Early Church in the ACTS OF THE APOSTLES and in Their Writings

CONTENTS

Introduction
  The Environment
  The People
  The Books
  The Expansion of Christianity

First Period
  The Church in Jerusalem from Pentecost to the persecution under Agrippa I (30-44 A.D.)

Second Period
  The mission of Paul to the Gentiles from the establishment of the Church in Antioch to the beginning of the persecution under Nero (44-64 A.D.)

Third Period
  The apostolic writings from the persecution under Nero till the death of St. John (64-104 A.D.)

Indexes

450 pages; $4.00 — SC0010

Papal and Conciliar Teachings on Scripture

Dei Verbum (Dogmatic Constitution on Divine Revelation)
Vatican II   25¢   EP0450Z

Divino Afflante Spiritu (The Promotion of Biblical Studies)
Pius XII   25¢   EP0970

The Historicity of the Gospels
Pontifical Biblical Commission   15¢   EP0552

Providentissimus Deus (On the Study of Sacred Scripture)
Leo XIII   25¢   EP0870

Spiritus Paraclitus (On the Fifteenth Centenary of the Death of St. Jerome)
Benedict XV   35¢   EP0487

Books About the Bible

Apostle to the Nations
The Life and Letters of St. Paul
Rev. Thomas W. Buckley, STD, SSL

Few, if any, have wielded as effectively as St. Paul that sword of the Spirit which is the Word of God (Eph. 6:17). Apostle of Jesus Christ, the thrust of his writings would keep at bay our ancient enemies. To beleaguered humanity they still afford hope in the face of tyranny, sin, and death. To enhance that hope through a deeper understanding of St. Paul's life and letters is the aim of this volume. It is meant for the general reader.
516 pages; cloth $15.00; paper $14.00 — SC0014

The Holy Gospel
Here is a unique Holy Gospel format—extra-large print; splendid commentary footnotes and illustrated throughout.
720 pages; cloth $6.00; paper $5.00 — SC0051

In the Light of the Bible (Vols. I & II)
Sr. Concetta Belleggia, DSP

"These little books present basic teachings for Catholic living in Christ and (as their title indicates) present them in the clear light of the written Word. Anyone interested in studying or teaching the Christ-life will find these books helpful and authoritative, because their authority rests on God's inspired Scripture."
—Most Rev. John F. Whealon, Archbishop of Hartford
Vol. I—141 pages; $2.00 — SC0060
Vol. II—117 pages; $2.00 — SC0061

The Lord Loves His People
Compiled by the Daughters of St. Paul

A unique book of prayers—all in the inspired words of the Psalms. 158 pages; plastic $5.00 — SC0085

Morality Today—The Bible in My Life
Daughters of St. Paul

A unique way to study the Ten Commandments in the light of the Bible! In simple and clear language, but with a very personal approach, each commandment is explained in all its aspects, negative and positive. We are invited to ponder... adore...and speak to God so that through instruction, reflection and prayer we may understand and love His holy Law.

All will find this book both informative and inspirational.
157 pages; cloth $3.25; paper $2.25 — SC0088

My Daily Gospel
Compiled by Rev. J. Robaldo, SSP

A Gospel passage for every day explained simply and applied to practical life situations by the Fathers and Doctors of the Church.

495 pages; paper $3.00 — SC0090

Archbishop Goodier's classic series on the life of Christ:
The Public Life of Our Lord Jesus Christ
(2 Volumes)
Most Rev. Alban Goodier, SJ

Among the most widely read and reread of all reconstructions of the story of the Son of Man.

With its unforgettable portrayal of Christ, its abundant and authentic materials, it is invaluable alike to those who preach and to all who desire to be a friend of Christ—which is the goal of the Christian vocation.

cloth $8.00 per volume; paper $7.00 per volume
cloth $15.95 per set; paper $13.95 per set.
Vol. I — SC0424; Vol. II — SC0425

The Passion and Death of Our Lord Jesus Christ
Most Rev. Alban Goodier, SJ

The author has guided his writing by some fundamental questions: "How does the passion reveal Christ to us? What manner of Man does He show Himself during that ordeal? What were His thoughts and feelings? And, hence,...what is the meaning of Jesus crucified to me here and now? Our main object is to study Him round whom the story is gathered, that, if we can, we may know Him the better." 424 pages; cloth $7.50; paper $5.95 — SC0423

Reading the Acts, Epistles and Revelation
J. Kingsley Dalpadado, OMI

Anyone interested in Scripture will find, along with hours of enjoyable reading, the results of the latest exegetical studies.

"The Gospels present to us what Paul calls 'the mystery of Christ.' The *Acts* and *Epistles* proclaim it, explain it and apply it to our daily lives. The Book of *Revelation,* written in a time of crisis and persecution, is a magnificent declaration of faith in this mystery which dominates history and transcends time."

432 pages; cloth $6.95; paper $5.95 — SC0431

Reading the Bible—A Guide to the Word of God for Everyone
J. Kingsley Dalpadado, OMI

Each chapter offers an introduction to a book of the Bible, giving background, setting and explanation, select passages for reading and thoughtful applications. Charts, quizzes, answer keys, suggested hymns and prayers, make this an ideal text for school, adult study, or individuals desirous of understanding Scripture better. 325 pages; cloth $5.95 — SC0430

Scriptural Meditations on the Rosary

Compiled by the Daughters of St. Paul
  Scriptural reflections to aid in meditating the mysteries.
92 pages; plastic $3.50 — MS0675

Spiritual Life in the Bible

Daughters of St. Paul
  A volume which pursues the truth about a wealth of timely and fundamental subjects.
  Written in a form of dialogue, the author continually draws from the Book of books—the Bible—whose Author is God, the Author of Truth and the true Light of the world.
  A book which will be of interest to both those who believe in objective truth, and those who honestly seek to pursue the truth. cloth $5.95; paper $4.00 — SC0445

The Study of Sacred Scripture

Cardinal Paul Y. Taguchi
  A concise study of Sacred Scripture: doctrinal aspects (Sacred Scripture, Tradition, Magisterium); present-day deviations; how Scripture should be read, studied, and explained.
71 pages; cloth $3.00; paper $2.00 — SC0446

Women of the Bible—Old Testament

Daughters of St. Paul
  Meet women who influenced the Patriarchs, Prophets, Judges and Kings of the Covenant of Old. Penetrate their hopes and dreams, struggles and sorrows. And you will see human nature writing its messages for every generation.
144 pages; cloth $5.95; paper $4.95 — SC0460

Women of the Gospel—New Testament

Daughters of St. Paul
  Profiles of 20 women found in the New Testament. Excellent complement to the book "Women of the Bible."
138 pages; cloth $5.95; paper $4.95 — SC0470

Words of Wisdom: A Proverb for Every Day

  A proverb for every day of the year interspersed with over 100 full-color pictures.
cloth $9.50 — SC0478

  Please order from addresses at the end of this book, specifying binding and item number, and allowing for postage. Thank you.

Daughters of St. Paul

IN MASSACHUSETTS
   50 St. Paul's Ave., Jamaica Plain, Boston, MA 02130;
     617-522-8911; 617-522-0875
   172 Tremont Street, Boston, MA 02111; **617-426-5464;
     617-426-4230**
IN NEW YORK
   78 Fort Place, Staten Island, NY 10301; **212-447-5071**
   59 East 43rd Street, New York, NY 10017; **212-986-7580**
   625 East 187th Street, Bronx, NY 10458; **212-584-0440**
   525 Main Street, Buffalo, NY 14203; **716-847-6044**
IN NEW JERSEY
   Hudson Mall — Route 440 and Communipaw Ave.,
     Jersey City, NJ 07304; **201-433-7740**
IN CONNECTICUT
   202 Fairfield Ave., Bridgeport, CT 06604; **203-335-9913**
IN OHIO
   2105 Ontario St. (at Prospect Ave.), Cleveland, OH 44115; **216-621-9427**
   25 E. Eighth Street, Cincinnati, OH 45202; **513-721-4838**
IN PENNSYLVANIA
   1719 Chestnut Street, Philadelphia, PA 19103; **215-568-2638**
IN VIRGINIA
   1025 King St., Alexandria, VA 22314
IN FLORIDA
   2700 Biscayne Blvd., Miami, FL 33137; **305-573-1618**
IN LOUISIANA
   4403 Veterans Memorial Blvd., Metairie, LA 70002; **504-887-7631;
     504-887-0113**
   1800 South Acadian Thruway, P.O. Box 2028, Baton Rouge, LA 70821
     504-343-4057; 504-343-3814
IN MISSOURI
   1001 Pine Street (at North 10th), St. Louis, MO 63101; **314-621-0346;
     314-231-1034**
IN ILLINOIS
   172 North Michigan Ave., Chicago, IL 60601; **312-346-4228
     312-346-3240**
IN TEXAS
   114 Main Plaza, San Antonio, TX 78205; **512-224-8101**
IN CALIFORNIA
   1570 Fifth Avenue, San Diego, CA 92101; **714-232-1442**
   46 Geary Street, San Francisco, CA 94108; **415-781-5180**
IN HAWAII
   1143 Bishop Street, Honolulu, HI 96813; **808-521-2731**
IN ALASKA
   750 West 5th Avenue, Anchorage AK 99501; **907-272-8183**
IN CANADA
   3022 Dufferin Street, Toronto 395, Ontario, Canada
IN ENGLAND
   128, Notting Hill Gate, London W11 3QG, England
   133 Corporation Street, Birmingham B4 6PH, England
   5A-7 Royal Exchange Square, Glasgow G1 3AH, England
   82 Bold Street, Liverpool L1 4HR, England
IN AUSTRALIA
   58 Abbotsford Rd., Homebush, N.S.W., Sydney 2140, Australia